The Collector's Encyclopedia Of

NIPPON PORCELAIN

Third Series

Joan F. Van Patten

COLLECTOR BOOKS
A Division of Schroeder Publishing Co., Inc.

Dedicated to the many collectors who helped make this book a reality!

Additional copies of this book may be ordered from:

Collector Books
P.O. Box 3009
Paducah, KY 42001

@ $24.95. Add $1.00 for postage and handling.

Copyright: Joan F. Van Patten, 1986
ISBN: 0-89145-308-3

Printed in Hong Kong by Everbest Printing Co. Ltd. for Four Colour Imports, Ltd., Louisville, Kentucky.

"A book is a book only when it is in the hands of a reader. The rest of the time it is an artifact."

William Sloane

And it is my hope that this edition of Nippon will be a well-used book by each owner and not merely an artifact. Read it. Glean Knowledge from it. But most of all, enjoy it!

Joan Van Patten

ACKNOWLEDGEMENTS

There were over fifty people who helped make Series III a reality. Some have contributed information, others a few photos and then there were friends and fellow collectors who contributed as many as 80 to 100 photographs. Hopefully every one of them is listed below; but, if not, please accept my apologies. This book is larger in scope than either of the first two and a "group" effort was truly necessary to bring it to readers.

First, I would like to thank my publisher, Bill Schroeder, who makes all these books possible and thanks also to Steve Quertermous, my editor at Collector Books. Without the "green light" from these two, the books would never have been undertaken.

Next, I want to thank my good friends, Bob and Flora Wilson, for the many, many beautiful photos they submitted. Bob took the pictures with loving care so that we could share their many treasures. I continually remarked about his expertise with the camera and he continually reassured me that he also has a huge stack of photo rejects at home. Norm and Marilyn Derrin are two more collectors who sent many photos of truly wonderful pieces of Nippon. They have a large and beautiful collection and I appreciate their sharing it with us. George Murphy was their photographer and deserves the credit for these great shots. George is also responsible for the chapter on photo tips which I hope will be of aid to collectors wanting to photograph and catalog their collections. Marie Young, my sister-in-law, took the photos of my items so that they could be shared with the readers of the book. Thanks, Marie.

Helen and Bob Karlin are to be thanked for the wonderful article on old salesmen's sample books from the Noritake Company. Their photographer, Azade Erhun, did a fantastic job capturing these wonderful pages. I am thrilled that we can finally share them with others in a book such as this. The discovery of these pages is very exciting and I am sure readers will share my enthusiasm once they view them.

My friend, Joan Oates, is responsible for the chapter on the Phoenix Bird pattern which is a subject that had been neglected in the previous Nippon books. Ken Oates photographed his wife's items and I wish to thank him for their inclusion. Joan is the specialist and expert in this field and she is also the author of books on the subject and editor of a newsletter for devotees of Phoenix Bird Chinaware. More information may be received from her about this pattern by writing to 5912 Kingsfield, W. Bloomfield, MI 48033.

Elyce Litts is the expert on Geisha Girl porcelain and she too has submitted a chapter for readers on her favorite subject. She is a contributor to several antique books and is author of many articles on this topic. She is the acknowledged expert in this area and the editor of a newsletter on the subject. Elyce may be reached by writing to P.O. Box 394, Morris Plains, NJ 07950. Thank you Joan and Elyce for your articles and accompanying photos.

My friends, Jess Berry and Gary Graves, sent me numerous photos of their wonderful Nippon collection. Jess also allowed me to reprint an article he wrote recently for the "INCC Newsletter" entitled "Pre-Nippon?." I feel it is an issue to which collectors may wish to give more thought and I want to thank him for his insight to this problem. My friend, Rachel Dolab, helped me with research and several of the passages from the early 1900 books were received from her. She was also kind enough to box up many pieces from her collection, bring them out to the house and allow us to photograph them.

Walt and Donna Ward photographed many items from their collection which they were anxious to share with others. The photographs were excellent and a definite asset to the book. Thank you both. My friends, Ken Harman and Bill Davis, have not only sent me numerous photos but have also helped me add to my personal collection. They manage to find some pretty terrific Nippon in their travels and both have added much to the field of Nipponing.

Linda Lau sent me many, many photos of her Nippon dolls along with descriptions and prices. Larry Strother was kind enough to photograph Linda's collection and I wish to thank him for the photos. These delightful dolls would enhance any collection. Joan Gilfillan and Paul Blessing, other collectors of Nippon dolls have completed the section on dolls with many from their collection. Thank you all.

Lee and Donna Call sent me numerous photos of the items in their extensive collection. They have all types of pieces and I was most anxious to include these photos in this publication. Other wonderful photos came from Kathy and Bob Wojciechowski. These two people have managed to amass a lovely collection over the years and their photos were a welcome addition. Sharon Endejan also helped with numerous photos and some important research work for which I am extremely greatful. Marjorie and Bill McEnelly also sent super photos of their collection. Bill has become quite the expert in taking photos and these too add so much to Series III.

Fred Tenney is a "dyed in the wool Nipponer" and over the years has been able to obtain many super pieces. He supplied a number of the photos used in the book. Linda Van Orden went so far as to send me her numerous photo albums so that I could pick and choose which photos to use. She also sent several items to be photographed. Thanks Linda. Stephen and Judy Costa photographed a number of pieces in their collection which definitely enhance this book.

Others I wish to thank for photos and/or information are Susan Garrison, Elaine Flaherty, Rita Gillis, Corrine Gould, Jean and Craig Cole, Mike and Grace Cole, Francile and John McLain, Larry Hartnell, Judy and Bill Boyd, Cathy Keyes, Roger Zeefe, Pauline Ross, Mary and Joseph Caliro, Janice Miles, Carol Audino, Jeanne Crowley, Kathy Murphy, Tom Burns, Ben Perez, Gil Corriveau, Viola Breves, Mel Mitchell, Gene Galloway, Lee Smith, Jan Thalberg, Leonard Taylor, Todd Lawrence and Rick Pence.

To those who helped with pricing I must say thank you a million times. It is a humongous task and one that takes complete concentration and a good knowledge about pricing and price trends. My good friends Bob Wilson, Rita Gillis, Ken Harman and Bill Davis worked diligently with me on this project and their imput was correlated, analyzed and finally assimilated to reflect the prices you will find in this revised guide. Carolyn and Larry Scherly gave pricing guidelines from Canada, Joan Gilfillan and Linda Lau helped with the doll section and Corrine Gould, Sharon Endejan and Roger Zeefe gave valued advice. Ultimately, though, the responsibility for the price guide fell on my shoulders so all criticism, comments and such are to be directed to me.

Thank you so much my good friends and fellow collectors. You have made another one of my dreams come true!

TABLE OF CONTENTS

INTRODUCTION

"On the day when man, walking upon the clayey soil, softened by inundations or rain, first observed that the earth retained the prints of his footsteps, the plastic art was discovered; and when lighting a fire to warm his limbs, or to cook his food, he remarked that the surface of the hearth changed its nature and its color, that the reddened clay became sonorous, impervious and hardened in its new shape, the art was revealed to him of making vessels fit to contain liquids."

Jacquemart

From the footprints of prehistoric man to the ceramic marvels of today, clay has left its mark on mankind. It seems that man, in every part of the world has been irresistibly led to seek a combination of both the useful as well as the beautiful when using clay.

There is found in a circa 1910 Ceramic Art Co. catalog, the following passage, "History is dumb as to the beginning of the potter's art, and often lapses into silence among the shifting nations of ancient years, the only record of their existence, extension and customs being in the clay treasures which time has spared. The potsherds which strew the path of civilization chronicle the progress of mankind, and show that races of remote and present times are 'kindred and allied by birth and made of the same clay.' In each of the older nations, the origin of the art is ascribed to those legendary beings - half divine, half human - who hover on the borderland of history; in each, its pottery reflects its religion and its customs, showing how art may embellish and perpetuate national life; and in the plastic relics of all, we find a worldwide record of the growth of intelligence and the expansion of artistic ideas.

"The crude savage, scratching an ornament on his coarse vase with a stick, and his modern successor working upon graceful forms of delicate fabric with brilliant colors, trained hand and cultivated taste, are both obeying the same impulse and following a universal and natural law.

"In all ages and climes - from that land whose aspiring pyramids reveal an antiquity surpassing record, to the forceful and progressive era of present life - the human family has loved to simulate Nature by conventionalizing her most beautiful handiwork. It has been held and maintained by the foremost exemplars of industrial art that conventional ornament was the only true form of creative decoration, and their claims are well sustained in those classic orders of architecture which have endured for centuries.

"Legend ascribes the invention of the potter's art in the 'land of Nippon' to Ooseitsumi, before the dawn of history, although the first accurate knowledge begins about the time of the Christian Era, when Nomino, a potter, by means of his art and wit, abolished a cruel custom - that of burying slaves with their dead masters. When the Empress died, Nomina quickly made images of earthenware, which he induced the Emperor to bury with her as substitutes for her favorite attendants. Humanity prevailed over custom, the absurd rite was abolished, and the potter rewarded by being allowed to take the surname Haji, artist in clay.

"Later, Haji and a Corean prince founded a potters' guild, and, it is said, made porcelain. However, accounts are contradictory, and it is quite likely that the secret of making translucent ware came to Japan from China. By conquest and diplomacy, the Japanese acquired from China and Corea the greater part of their ceramic knowledge, which they gradually absorbed and transmuted, building up an individual and national art. The best and noblest of the Japanese were artists, and engaged in pursuits which in China were relegated to mechanical workmen. These potter-princes give us individual creations wrought with marvelous skill. Artistic ability was recognized by titles of honor; and the prevalence of hereditary occupations provided for the transmission of technical skill."

The Nippon porcelain we collect and cherish today is of such fine quality that it will literally last through the ages, even for a thousand years. It can be the beginning of a timeless heritage and who can begin to guess how many generations to come will see and love it as collectors do today. The word Nippon is synonomous with the word Japan, the Land of the Rising Sun, and so it is that the rays from this Japanese sun continue to light up the lives of so many Nippon enthusiasts.

It was not necessary for items entering the United States prior to 1891 to be backstamped with their country of origin. However, in October of 1890, the McKinley Tariff Act was passed by Congress and stated the following:

"That on and after the first day of March, eighteen hundred and ninety-one, all articles of foreign manufacture, such as are usually or ordinarily marked, stamped, branded or labeled, and all packages containing such or other imported articles, shall, respectively, be plainly marked, stamped, branded or labeled in legible English words, so as to indicate the country of their origin; and unless so marked, stamped, branded or labeled they shall not be admitted to entry."

Thus the Nippon era began, lasting until 1921 when the government reversed its position and decided that Nippon was a Japanese word, the English equivalent of which was Japan. Customs agents were then instructed that as of September 1, 1921, merchandise from Japan, the marking of which was governed by this provision, would not be released when bearing only the Japanese word "Nippon" to indicate the country of origin. Items made after this period were to be marked "Japan" or "Made in Japan."

Research indicates though that not all imported goods were marked as dictated by the law. There were loopholes in the law which allowed for some unmarked items to enter this country. For instance, at some ports of entry, goods were allowed into the country if merely the box or container was stamped with the name of the country of origin. Novice collectors would probably fare better by purchasing only marked pieces as it is sometimes difficult to distinguish between genuine Nippon era items and the later Japanese wares. Marked items have considerably more resale value but I have seen "marked" items that were poorly executed on inferior porcelain and not worthy to be added to any collection. An item that is well made and decorated should not be rejected merely for its lack of mark but collectors must accept the fact that the price it will sell for later on will generally be considerably lower than that of a marked piece.

Because so many new items have been located recently and new information has been uncovered, Series III has been produced and is intended to be a continuation of the first two books. Readers will find basic information and photos of color plates numbered 1 to 366 in the first book and plate numbers 367 to 1210 in Series II.

This particular volume contains many new marks, more news on the reproductions flooding the market, old ads, photo tips, dinnerware patterns, techniques used on these wares and much, much more.

Be a knowledgeable collector. Study your subject in detail. Read all the books and articles on Nippon that you can. It is my wish that this particular volume on Nippon porcelain will help make new things familiar and familiar things new to you.

Visit as many antique shows and flea markets as possible. Ask questions of both dealers and collectors. Get to know your Nippon. Remember, an education is what you can get from reading the fine print in advance and an experience is often what you get from not reading it.

MANUFACTURE AND DECORATION

We can all appreciate the beauty of Nippon porcelain but just how was it manufactured and decorated? It's sad for most collectors to find out that most of these records are not available. They were either lost through the years or destroyed in World War II. It has been an almost impossible task for researchers to acquire information; however, I was fortunate to find an old catalog of the Ceramic Art Co. of Trenton, New Jersey, circa 1910. Besides depicting pieces available for decoration, the book tells how the wares were manufactured and decorated. Most likely the Japanese utilized some of these same techniques. Let me share with you some of the interesting passages of this catalog.

"Part of the preparations for porcelain-making take place before the materials reach the potter; but most of the ingredients come to the factory in their raw state and are there calcined and ground as the different 'bodies' and 'glazes' demand. The time necessary for grinding varies from hours to weeks, according to the different articles, but all the earthy substances must be reduced to an impalable powder and cleared from any particles of iron or other foreign substances. The pulverized materials, mixed in proper proportion, are now ready for the 'blungers' or vats, in which they are 'blunged' in water, so as to form a uniform cream-like mass, called 'slip,' which now goes into the mixing pans, is drawn off, and after being sifted through fine silken lawn, is ready for the 'caster.' These purely mechanical operations require the closest attention, as the fine quality of the ware depends on the knowledge and care exercised in the mixing room - the potter's laboratory.

"The next point of interest is the clay-shop, where all the forms are modeled and cast. From the clay model a 'block mould' in two exactly fitting portions, is made of plaster of Paris and carefully preserved. From this 'block mould' a 'case' is made, that is, a plaster replica of the model, and from this case, in turn, as many working moulds as may be required. Modeling and mould-making demand not only knowledge, skill and time, but foresight and experience, as the modeler must allow for shrinkage in firing (about one-seventy of the size) and guard against the use of forms that will warp or sink in the fire. Handles, tops of vases, stands and bases, are all modeled and cast separately, so that one piece of ware may require four or five moulds. Besides the moulds used in casting, it is necessary to make many devices, such as rings and stands to hold certain forms in shape while undergoing the fire.

"The caster binds together the two portions of the mould, sets it upon his wheel, to which he gives a deft turn, and pours in the slip. If the piece he is making is to be small and thin, he leaves the slip in the mould but a moment, then quickly pours out all that has not adhered to it; a thicker article requires a proportionately longer time. The sponge-like plaster readily absorbs the water in the slip, leaving a shell of clay, which, as it dries, shrinks away from the mould, while it retains its shape. The mould containing the embryo ware is then set in the 'drying-room' until the clay shell is hard enough to be handled. When sufficiently dry and firm, each piece of 'green ware' is removed from the mould and set upon the wheel by skillful fingers; superfluous edges are trimmed and 'finished,' the various parts are cemented together by slip, and the pieces, overgrown and sallow-looking, are arranged on a long board which a level-headed person carries downstairs to the kiln-shed.

" 'Placing' or 'packing' and 'firing' a kiln are very important, although apparently simple processes, for on the watchfulness and experience of the fireman depends much of the success of the potter. The ware to be burned is placed for protection and convenience in fire-clay boxes, called 'seggars' or 'saggers,' in which it rests on sand or flint, many shapes requiring regular beds of this material. A strip or 'wad' of moist clay is then laid around the top of the seggar and it is placed in the kiln close to the side, another seggar is set on the first, and so on to the crown of the kiln, each of these upright tiers being called a 'bung.' The 'wads' are to further protect the ware from the fumes and smoke and to steady the 'bung.' When the kiln is full, the door is bricked up and plastered over with clay, and the fire started.

"The kiln is a bee-hive-shaped structure of red brick, lined with fire-brick, and generally about sixteen feet in diameter inside and about the same height to the 'crown.' Above this crown or ceiling, the walls narrow as they go upward. The brick walls of the kiln are bound by heavy iron hoops or girdles to give greater strength. Around the base at equal distances are the fire-holes, eight or more in number, communicating with the interiour by openings above and below. The length of time required for a biscuit fire varies according to the body and composition of the ware, from twenty-four to a hundred hours.

"When the kiln has cooled and the ware, now 'biscuit,' is removed, a transformation has taken place; the friable, clay-colored articles are now beautifully white, firm, translucid pieces of porcelain - that is, unless one of those frequent and mysterious misfortunes, which constantly assail the poor potter, has distorted and discolored a portion of them.

"The biscuit now goes to the biscuit-wareroom, where it is carefully selected, each separate piece is rubbed with sand-stone, polished with sand-paper and brushed until it is perfectly smooth and absolutely free from dust; it is then ready for the dipping room. The glaze of glass-forming compound is prepared with great care. Most of the ingredients, in due proportion, are first melted together, forming a 'fritt,' which is finely ground and mixed with the other necessary materials. All are now ground together in water until the mass forms a heavy, creamy liquid; into this solution the dipper plunges the pieces of ware, giving it a skillful shake and turn to distribute the coating evenly and avoid a superfluity. It is then set on the 'rack' to dry, and carefully guarded from dust and foreign substances. When dry, the ware has its second burning in the glost kiln - a fire of lesser heat (for soft porcelain) than the biscuit fire. Placing the glost kiln is a work of even more care than the biscuit requires. Each seggar must be 'washed' with a special glaze, pieces must not touch one another or the sides of the seggar. Flat pieces are set on fire-clay 'pins.' Stilts are also used to keep certain articles apart. The arrangement in 'bungs' is the same as before, and the degree of heat required is tested by means of small clay rings, called 'trials,' put through other small openings, called 'spy-holes,' the interior of the kiln may be seen when the fire is at white heat, glowing with such incandescence that an ordinary observer cannot distinguish any tangible objects therein. When the experienced fireman is satisfied with the condition of things inside, the warm work of 'drawing' the kiln begins; the glowing coals are raked out of the fire-holes and the hose is turned on. After the kiln has cooled, and the seggars are opened, the ware is critically examined and the perfect results of these various processes are stored in their 'bins' in the 'white-ware room.' The imperfect results - always too many in spite of every care and caution, are ruthlessly broken. Any purchaser inclined to complain of high prices should visit the mound of 'potsherds' outside every pottery, mute witness to the wide range of disaster in this industry.

"The decoration of pottery and porcelain is an art of infinite restrictions and uncertainties, but of never-failing fascination. The many styles of embellishment may be divided into two great classes, based on the manner of application - overglaze and underglaze.

"Underglaze decoration, properly speaking, is painted on either the 'green' ware or biscuit, after which the piece is glazed and subjected to the glost fire. Comparatively few colors will bear this 'hard fire,' the principal ones, sufficiently strong, being blue, brown, green and yellow. A style of monochrome painting which, properly executed, gives most beautiful results, is miscalled 'underglaze,' because the 'hard fire' colors are used. No accurate name has been invented, although 'over-underglaze' and 'interglaze' are fairly descriptive. The color, finely ground and lawned, is mixed with various oils and spirits and applied to the glazed surface of the ware, exactly as a wash-drawing would be made. The piece is dried in the kiln for enamel colors, and sent a second time into the glost fire, where the color penetrates the glaze, becoming part of it. The danger of loss in this process is not only the same as for the glazed ware, but presents an additional uncertainty; a 'short fire' leaves the color raw and cold, while a degree of heat greater than that of the first glost fire causes the glaze to flow, and as the color cannot penetrate the vitreous body, it moves with the glaze. Thus, an elaborate decoration often 'runs' beyond recognition, and the whole piece is lost. Few pieces painted in this manner are completely satisfactory in one firing, so that every finished article has generally passed through four 'hard fires' and two enamel fires, - six times through the kiln in all, often many more. The results, however, justify the labor, as the decoration, apart from its artistic possibilities, becomes a part of the object, is absolutely unharmed by friction or acids and can be destroyed only by fracture.

"Overglaze decoration admits of greater variety in color and manipulation and is attended with less risk, although here also the greatest care must be exercised from the grinding of the color to the final 'burnishing.' A kiln of different construction is required for firing, and the degree of heat and time of burning varies with different colors.

"The successful combination of vitrifiable colors in a polychrome decoration depends not only on the artist's intuition, but also on the china painter's knowledge of color chemistry. He is often obliged to resort to a method not unlike lithography, of doing portions of his work one at a time, and if gold or raised paste enters into his design, he must always wait until the rest is fired before that is applied. The ceramic artist, more than any other, must, from the beginning of his efforts, see with his mind's eye his completed work, and with infinite patience await the result of the 'fiery trial.' A more mechanical process of decoration is that of printing the design in color or gold, and afterward touching up with the pencil. This is a much quicker method than hand work, and often very effective.

"Fashions in ceramic ornamentation come and go in popular favor, while the standard of excellence grows higher each year, as culture is more widely diffused. No producer of beautiful and useful things strives more earnestly than does the potter to win and deserve a name and fame from an appreciative public."

TECHNIQUES USED ON NIPPON WARES

As stated in the introduction, it is my hope in Series III to make new things familiar and familiar things new. Collectors very often talk about a particular type of ware such as wedgwood pieces. They know what these items look like and vaguely know how they were manufactured; but few have ever really taken a good, close look at these pieces. Sometimes we gain a new perspective on our collectibles when we study them a little more in detail.

The majority of Nippon-era wares are hand painted to some degree. Some are completely hand painted while others have only a little hand painting added for the finishing touches; and, of course, there are those that utilize decals or decalcomanias for the entire design. Collectors will find that portraits are usually decals as the fine detail work would be almost impossible to duplicate on a mass scale. The decals are used for part of the artwork; the trim and moriage or beadwork is usually added and compliments the decal. Although most items which are decorated with decals do not command the higher price of the hand painted wares, the portraits are one of the exceptions to the rule. They are very much in demand with collectors and if the accompanying handwork is of superior quality, the price can be very hefty.

A good magnifying glass can be an aid to the collector in identifying which is which. A decal will always look like a series of dots under the magnifying glass whereas the hand painted piece will show the brush strokes.

A number of Nippon pieces are found with all-over beading while others will have just a trim of bead work. The earlier made items were produced by applying clay slip to actually make tiny "beads" on the item. After firing, the "beads" were enameled over with gold or other colors. Many of the later pieces, however, merely had dots of enameling applied to acquire this effect. When more and more items were manufactured, mass production techniques were utilized to cut down on the time being spent on each. It was determined that the "beading" effect could be achieved almost as well with dots of enamel and the time saved could be used on other items.

BEADING

CLOISONNE' ON PORCELAIN

Another unusual type of decoration to be found on Nippon-marked pieces is cloisonné on porcelain. Many times it will look like a mosaic pattern, set stones or tree bark.

The decoration was originally divided into cells called cloisons and the cloisons were separated by strips of soft metal which kept the colors separated during firing. The metal also often outlined shapes such as fruit, butterflies, and flowers. Upon firing, the enamel and metal fused to the body of the item. These items resemble other cloisonné pieces except that they are produced on porcelain rather than the traditional metal background.

Collectors should note that submerging the pieces in water can dislodge the cloisons from the background and this manner of cleaning should be discouraged.

CORALENE

Most of the coralene pieces that collectors will find are not marked with Nippon as country of origin but have a Japan backstamp. The coralene pieces that are back-stamped Nippon generally have a rising sun in their backstamp along with the initials RS.

Coralene items were produced by firing small colored beads on the pieces giving them a plush velvety look. This vitreous coating of beads is often found in the shapes of flowers, birds, etc.

Years ago the most popular pattern of coralene on glass items was one of seaweed and coral, hence the name **coral**ene was given to this type of design.

Japanese coralene on porcelain was patented by Alban L. Rock, an American living in Yokohama in 1909. A complete copy of the patent can be found in *The Collector's Encyclopedia of Nippon Porcelain, Series II.*

GOLD OVERLAY

When gold decoration is heavily applied to a Nippon item, collectors refer to this as gold overlay. Many of these pieces are found with a cobalt background but it is not impossible to find this type of decoration on other wares. The gold was fired separately on these articles after all the other decoration had been completed. Gold melts at a much lower temperature than other colors and it would have melted into the other decoration if fired at too high a temperature. If the potter overfired the piece, the gold would become discolored; hence pieces decorated in this manner had to be treated with extreme care.

INCISED DECORATION

Incised pieces of Nippon were produced while the clay body of the item was still in a state of soft clay. At this time, pointed tools were used to carve out a design. This, too, is an unusual type of decoration to find on Nippon wares but the Japanese seemed capable of producing and imitating all types.

MORIAGE

Most of the moriage decoration we find on Nippon wares is the result of the slip trailing of liquified clay on an item to make a design. Slip trailing could be applied before or after glazing and today, we can find items decorated in a myriad of colors; however, white moriage trim is found more than any of the other colors. Dragons, lacy designs and the wheat pattern are among the most popular with collectors. Tubing was filled with softened clay slip and the decorating was done much as we would trim a cake today. However, the body of the articles had to be in a state of firm moist clay or the decoration might have fallen off or cracked when it dried. A few of the Nippon era moriage pieces, however, were decorated by hand rolling and shaping the clay and then applying it to the item.

Collectors will find that a portion of moriage wares are not backstamped, which may mean that they possibly pre-date the Nippon period, post date it or perhaps were never marked; or a paper label could have been originally affixed which has been washed off over the years. Collectors must exercise their judgment when selecting unmarked pieces. The quality of the porcelain and its decoration should be heavily weighed before purchase.

One of the most popular patterns is that of the jeweled-eyed slip-trailed dragon. Many of the wares bearing this pattern are unmarked and most of the ones that are backstamped have been found bearing marks #47, #52 and #71. Mark #47 is the M in wreath mark. Items backstamped with this mark were manufactured by the famous Noritake Co. in Nagoya, Japan, for export to the United States. The "M" stands for Morimura (the Morimura Bros. were the forerunners of the Noritake

Co.) and the wreath was designed from the crest of the Morimuras. The manufacture of items with this particular backstamp began in 1911. The Noritake Co. believes that the country of origin, "Nippon," was changed in this mark to "Made in Japan" as early as 1918; however, they have no record to show the date the new mark was registered. The Noritake Co. cannot trace whether the green M in wreath mark is the old one or not. The M in wreath mark is the one Nippon collectors will find the most often. Over 50% of our Nippon-era wares are found bearing this backstamp.

Mark #52 is the familiar maple leaf mark which was used by the Morimura Bros. who later founded the Noritake Co. It was first used in 1891, and can possibly date until 1921. The Noritake Co. has been a big help with research, but they are severely hampered as most of their records were destroyed during World War II. I am constantly seeking answers to Nippon-era Noritake pieces as well as the later ones manufactured in the 1921-41 period; but it is a good guess that we may NEVER find out all the answers.

Mark #71 is the pagoda mark and not related to the Noritake Co. in any way that we are aware. Research does not reveal any information on this particular mark. There were so many individual companies producing china in Japan during this time span that it has been virtually impossible to find out about all of them.

The dragon pattern items are very much in demand by a number of collectors. Price depends on condition, rarity, etc., as there are many variables that play a part in determining the cost of an article.

Moriage decoration is found in a "raised" appearance, usually the result of the slip trailing of liquified clay on the item to make the design. Collectors should be careful not to confuse this type of work with pieces that are molded in relief (blown-out) which have a raised appearance due to the particular mold used when manufacturing the item.

PATTERN STAMPED DECORATION

Pattern-stamped decoration is accomplished by using a special stamp or roller which has a design cut into it. This is pressed onto the soft body of a clay piece and the design emerges in low relief.

This type of work generally results in an impressed motif of a repeated pattern.

RELIEF MOLDED ITEMS

Relief molded pieces are made in ONE piece and are not to be confused with items that have sprigged-on decoration or those with moriage decor.

Molded-in-relief Nippon items are also referred to by collectors as "blown-out." This term, however, is a misnomer as the items are not blown-out but the design does protrude out from the background. The design was incised in the mold and when the clay slip was poured in, it filled the cut out areas. Thus, the pattern was embossed on the item by the mold in which the item was shaped. These items all appear to have had some type

of upward pressure from the underside.

The pieces have a three-dimensional appearance which ranges from high relief, where the figures stand out more than half their implied thickness, to half relief, right down to low relief, where the figure is just slightly raised.

SILVER OVERLAY

Collectors do not easily locate items having a decoration of silver overlay as they are unusual to find. A heavy application of silver trim decorates these wares and collectors must exercise care when cleaning these pieces as they can be damaged. The items will tarnish but harsh abrasives should never be used to clean them.

Like gold, silver was different in make-up from other glazes and had to be handled differently. Silver melts at a much lower temperature than the other colors used and the manufacturer had to fire the silver separately.

SPONGE TAPESTRY

The term "sponge tapestry" puts most collectors at a loss in trying to describe this type of ware. All the pieces found to date have a front panel that has a pitted appearance looking almost like a sponge, hence the name sponge tapestry. These items are unlike tapestry pieces because of their irregular texture. The area is decorated with flowers or a scene and is usually surrounded with heavy gold trim.

SPRIGGED-ON DECORATION

Sprigged-on decoration is achieved by applying small molded pieces to the surface of a clay item using slip or liquid clay.

Two or more pieces are necessary for this type of work and it differs from relief molded items where the decoration is molded right on the item.

The decoration is made in a small press mold. After it is removed from the mold, the back is moistened with clay slip and it is attached to the piece. Both the item and decoration need to have the same degree of shrinkage or the decoration may crack off during firing or even before.

TAPESTRY

The tapestry technique used on Nippon wares is similar to that of the Royal Bayreuth pieces. The textured surface found on the item was not produced in the mold but after the pieces had been cast. Material was dipped in porcelain slip and soaked, then spread on the artisan's hands and the excess patted out. This material was then stretched onto the item and bisque fired. During the firing, the material burned off, leaving a textured surface on the piece, often resembling needlepoint or tapestry. The item was then painted and fired again in the usual manner.

This technique produced some novel textured effects on pieces. Sometimes the item will look as though a coarsely woven cloth had been used while another will look as though a linen material was utilized. Some pieces are completely covered with the tapestry texture while others may only have a reserve or border of tapestry decoration.

ADVERTIQUES AND

PROMOTIONAL ITEMS

Collectors not only collect unusual techniques on Nippon wares, but many make a speciality out of some of the unusual categories available. Advertising items or so-called "advertiques" were often made quite inexpensively and because of this, collectors will find that the quality on these wares is sometimes inferior to other pieces. Advertiques had messages printed on them such as the combination matchbox holder and ashtray advertising Fatima brand cigarettes. Others found have the original sticker from Morimura Bros. of New York City which says "Compliments of Morimura Bros." and there are those that say "Compliments of Eastern Outfitting Co."

These items were originally given away or sold for very little to promote the company or product involved. They are difficult to find as so many were originally thrown out and the price on these small pieces generally reflects their scarcity.

Back in the early 1900's, Japanese items were imported into the United States in staggering quantities. They were sold virtually everywhere, the five and ten cent stores, through mail order catalogs, grocery stores, gift shops, etc. They were inexpensive to purchase and it gave the middle class the opportunity to enjoy many of the things previously available only to the rich. Today these advertiques and promotional items can make for an interesting hobby. They can be a good starting point for collectors and since most are small in size, they're good for those with limited space.

One of my researchers has the small Nippon nappy in her collection which is featured in Series I, plate #131. It bears the M in wreath backstamp plus the words "Fair Week 1912, The D.M. Read Co., Bridgeport, Conn." She called the D.M. Read Co. and received the following information:

"The D.M. Read Co. had an annual Houseware's Fair to which tradesmen, vendors and salespeople were invited. They were presented with commemorative items made for the occasion including specialty pieces of china which were dated and which specified 'Fair Week' on them. The general public, of course, attended because it was a big sale but only the tradesmen, vendors or salespeople were the recipients of these particular china items."

**Fatima Turkish Cigarettes
Combination matchbox holder and ashtray**

GOLD ETCHED

Years ago, many of the Nippon pieces were imported into the United States as "in-the-white" blanks. An old Thayer and Chandler catalog, circa 1918, featured a number of Nippon blanks which were "acid etched china for encrusted gold decoration." The company suggested that ceramists use Hubbard Roman Gold all over the china to achieve the gold etched effect.

The famous Pickard Co. also imported many of the Nippon "in-the-white" items and collectors may possibly find some of these today containing the dual backstamp of both Nippon and Pickard. The Pickard decorating studio, now the Pickard China Co., had many artists on their staff, several from Chicago's famous Art Institute. Pickard-decorated Nippon wares are desirable among collectors and many are even artist-signed which increases their price and collectibility. The Pickard Co. produced this design on their items by applying two coats of gold to the etched item.

GOUDA IMITATIONS

Pieces which are decorated in a style imitative of the Gouda wares are unlike any of the other Nippon wares. These items were styled after the pottery wares of South Holland which were very popular in the early 1920's. Gouda items are vivid in color and were influenced by the Art Nouveau period.

NOVELTIES

Novelty items are another area a few collectors are pursuing and prices do seem to have risen in this category quite quickly.

Novelty pieces cover a broad collecting field and among the most popular are the figural items. Although the word figural is not listed in my dictionary, my interpretation is that it is a utilitarian item that either has a relief figure attached for ornamentation or the piece is in the shape of a figure that is utilitarian by itself.

Some of the favorites are the night lights which were molded in the shape of an owl, rabbit, Dutch girl, eagle, etc. There is also a souvenir pin dish with the ever popular Nipper, symbolic of the RCA Corporation.

Figural ashtrays are a rarity but known ones include those displaying the kingfisher, seal, penguins, dogs, etc. Minature Dutch shoes are sought after, also figural incense burners and bookends. In this field, some new things keep appearing each day.

PORTRAITS

Portrait items are very much in demand with Nippon collectors and this is reflected in their price. The majority employ the use of decals for the decoration and these same decals can be found on items marked R.S. Prussia, Germany, etc. Many of the portraits are of Victorian ladies.

SOMETSUKE

Sometsuke decoration consists of an underglaze of blue and white. Many times the mythological phoenix or ho·o bird is featured on these pieces. The willow pattern is another favorite. A common backstamp found on these items is that of Royal Sometuke (notice the difference in spelling).

SOUVENIR ITEMS

A number of Nippon items will be found which were once souvenirs. A favorite with collectors are those having a decal of the Capital Building in Washington, D.C. on them. This particular decalcomania portrays the Capitol at the turn of the century.

Others are found that are souvenirs of Miami, Florida, or Newport, Rhode Island, Saratoga, New York, etc. Most are small in size and can make for an interesting collection; however, it must be noted that many are not always of the finest quality porcelain.

WEDGWOOD

The wedgwood decoration found on Nippon is an imitation of Josiah Wedgwood's popular Jasper ware pieces. Most of the Nippon wares are found having a light blue background with white moriage slip trailed decoration while there are some that have a green background or even a rare lavender color. The colors can also be found in reverse.

The wedgwood look was usually accomplished by means of slip trailing liquid clay on the item, other times by means of sprigging on small ornamentation. The wedgwood pattern found on Nippon wares can be that of an all-over covering or just as a border or trim with a scenic or floral decor.

NIPPON PATTERNS, STYLES AND SHAPES

Many collectors have difficulty describing their Nippon wares. Nippon is found in so many shapes and with so many different patterns that it would be a full-time job to place a descriptive name on each but many patterns are repeated on a number of pieces and have acquired various titles to describe them over the years.

The dictionary describes "to spot" something as "to watch for, take note of, recognize, detect and to discover." In 1983 a small group of Nippon enthusiasts undertook a comprehensive study of Nippon-era pieces to help themselves and others describe their items. The

SPOTTER was published as an aid in identifying the numerous and varied patterns, designs and shapes found on these wares. In fact the title, SPOTTER, derives its name from Styles, Patterns, Ornamentation, Techniques, Transfers, Examples and Reproductions. All references are to Collector's Encyclopedia of Nippon Porcelain, Series I, II & III. Many, but not necessarily all, examples of each pattern listed are given. This listing follows and should prove to be valuable to both collectors and dealers when buying or advertising a piece of Nippon.

Nippon was produced in many patterns, designs and styles which were imitative of other popular wares.

Many of our **portraits** are identifiable:

There are a number of hanging plaques found in a **series**:

Plate No.

Vase shapes found:

Examples of **different handles** found:

Examples of different **kinds of feet**:

INFORMATION GLEANED FROM OTHER SOURCES

Information is often gathered from many sources and in my quest for knowledge about Nippon porcelain, I checked old catalog ads, the National Archives, old newspaper articles, old books and travel guides. They have all given me a better insight into Japan and the ceramic industry which flourished there in the late 1800's and early 1900's. The following is an excerpt from a 1914 travel guide to Japan:

"Ceramics (Greek: potters' clay; a piece of pottery, etc.) occupy one of the most important places in Japanese art products, and the pottery industry dates from remote, pre-historic times. The fictile arts appeal strongly to the modern craftsmen and by them they have been elevated to an unusually high degree of artistic excellence.

"The first pottery which history takes note of in Japan is the *Kameoka*-ware, — a crude, unglazed, and undecorated ware supposed to be the rude artistic expression of the autochthons of the country, and exhumed in considerable quantities in the *Kameoka* region of N. Japan. The forms are awkward, inclining to spherical shapes, and the surface decorations of the best pieces confined to elementary diapers of straight lines or curves, scratched in the clay when soft with a pointed tool. *Captain Brinkley* points out the significant fact that the ornamentation of some of the 'pilgrim-bottles' (a form so common to the early pottery of many nations) bears no resemblance to the decorations followed in China and Korea, but strongly resembles that constantly adopted by the potters of Greece and Cyprus in ancient times. 'This close affiliation to Apulian and Cypriote decorations suggests an interesting range of speculation, implying, as it does, a pronounced racial distinction between the dolmen-building Japanese and the inhabitants of the near-by Asiatic continent.' The early potters occupied a very low place of intelligence, and possessed neither artistic ability nor independent creative power. They were apparently unable to produce anything more complex than lightly burned terra-cotta and hard-burned earthenware similar to that made by the aboriginal potters of the S.W. of the U.S. They seem to have understood the use of the wheel and had a crude conception of decorative effects, but they knew nothing of translucid porcelain, and were not able to apply glaze to their wares. Oddly enough, they appear to have had no acquaintance with the decorative motives which are so intimately associated with Chinese applied art — dragons, phoenixes, tigers, the key-pattern, the fylfot, elaborate diapers, etc. Unlike the history of pottery-making in Mexico (where the art attained a high development as long as it remained uninfluenced by foreign ideas, but which degenerated and declined after the Spanish invasion), the Mongoloid intruders in Japan enriched the art with so many ideas and designs that its influence is now felt in almost every corner of the world.

"When *Gyogi* came to Japan from Korea in the middle of the 8th cent., he gave such an impetus to pottery-making that many native antiquarians regard him as the founder of the art in Japan. 'His figure assumed such historical importance that everything antecedent passed out of view, and to this day, whenever from any long-unexplored place, there is exhumed a specimen of unsightly and time-stained pottery, it is unhesitatingly christened *"Gyogi-yaki"* ' (*Gyogi*-ware). Up to the 12th cent. the production of glazed earthenware was limited, and the finest existing pieces dating from the years preceding were manifestly of Chinese (or Korean) origin. About 1223 *Kato Shirozœmon* (or *Kagemasa*), a native potter (now known as the father of pottery in Japan) who had achieved some local distinction, went to China to study the development of the art in the Middle Kingdom; returning 6 yrs. later he settled at Seto, in Owari Province, and began the production of a ware which to-day is held in high esteem. The workmanship was superior to anything that had hitherto been produced; the paste was reddish-brown clay, with a considerable admixture of silicious particles, and the glaze, applied with no mean skill, was most commonly dark brown with occasional streaks or patches of a different tint. The chief productions were tea-jars of various shapes and sizes, which, having been from the very first treasured with great care by their fortunate possessors, are still to be found, but are held at fabulous prices. So great a reputation did this *Toshiro-yaki* (as the ware was commonly called) enjoy, and such prestige did its appearance give to the potters of Owari, that most everything which preceded it was considered unworthy, and the name *Seto-mono* (Seto goods or things) thenceforth became the generic term for all ceramic manufactures in Japan, just as are *Talavera* in Spain, *Delft* in Holland, and *China* in Europe.

"There is now scarcely a province in the Empire where pottery, faience, stoneware, or porcelain is not produced; most of the products are attractive and some are exceedingly beautiful. As a rule they are not designated according to their character, but their origin, as: *Satsuma*-ware, *Kutani-yaki*; *Seto-mono*; *Hizen*-ware, *Kyoto*-ware, etc. The designations *Ishi-yaki* for hard-burned resonant porcelain and stoneware, and *Tsuchi-yaki* for softer earthenwares, however, are known and accepted everywhere. Porcelain[1] (which was invented by the Chinese) stands at the head as the noblest member of the family of ceramics, and large quantities are made and exported to different parts of the world. As a book would be necessary to catalogue all the wares now made in Japan, only those with which most travelers are familiar, and with which they usually come in contact when in Japan, will be mentioned here. Porcelainists will find a wealth of valuable data, supplemented by many handsome illustrations in *Rein's Industries of Japan,* and *Brinkley's Oriental Series.*

"(a) THE WARES OF KYOTO are legion, and in its 400 or more kilns the sometime Imperial capital produces ordinary pottery, faience, and porcelain in almost endless variety. With the exception perhaps of Yokohama, no Japanese city contains porcelain shops that are such a sustained delight to collectors and where such varied and attractive stocks are carried. The district lying along the W. flank of *Higashi-yama,* from *Konkozan's* pottery in *Awata* to *Kiyomizu-dera* and beyond, is studded with glowing kilns and rows of porcelain shops, while hundreds of the latter are scattered throughout the broad city. The wares are usually divided into four classes: *Raku-yaki* (p. ccliv); *Awata-yaki, Iwakura-yaki* (which to the casual eye is almost indistinguishable from the *Awata* ware), and *Kiyomizu-yaki.* Although history records that the first Kyoto potter, *Unrin-in Yasuhito,* the 7th son of the *Emperor Nimyo,* lived and worked during the 9th cent., the art acquired but little importance before the 16th cent., when the *Raku faience inaugurated by the Korean Ameya* became a favorite ware with the Kyoto tea-clubs. Distinctively Japanese, *Raku-yaki* is now made in many parts of the country. It is a coarse and somewhat clumsy ware of a brittle light-colored *pate* covered with black (the staple type), yellow, red, white, or salmon glaze easily recognized by its peculiarly opaque, waxy appearance; and sometimes gilded, but more often curiously speckled and pitted with red. It is much esteemed by Japanese, particularly that made at Kyoto by the descendants (in the 13th generation) of the founder (upon whom *Hideyoshi* conferred a gold seal bearing the symbol *Raku,* whence the trademark).

"*Nomura Seisuke,* who with his wares is known to posterity as *Ninsei,* and who (in the middle of the 17th cent.), after learning the valuable secrets of the old Hizen workshops at *Arita,* produced the first vitrifiable enameled ware in Kyoto, is regarded as the founder of the industry in the old metropolis. His first productions were potted in the district of *Omuro,* at a kiln called *Otowa,* whence the term *Omuro-yaki,* by which the early pieces are known. Later he worked at factories called *Awata, Iwakura,* and *Mizoro.* On the slope of *Otowa-yama,* which is now crowned by the *Kiyomizu* temple, is the celebrated *Kiyomizu-zaka,* which soon after *Ninsei's* time became, and has remained, a center for the manufacture of ceramics. *Awata,* where the *Kinkozan* potteries are located, is about ½ M. to the N.; *Mizoro* is 4 M. to the N.W. of this, and *Iwakura* 2½ M. N. of *Mizoro.* The remarkably rapid development of the Kyoto faience during the latter half of the 17th cent. is largely due to the impetus given to it by *Ninsei.* 'In his hands it became an object of rare beauty. The surface of choice specimens of his handiwork conveys the

impression of being covered with very fine netting, rather than with a tracery of intersecting lines. Its appearance is aptly described by the Chinese term 'fish-roe crackle.' His monochrome glazes are scarcely less remarkable. He produced many charming tints, and his skill as a modeler was scarcely less than his mastery of mechanical details. There is no name more renowned in the catalogue of Japanese ceramists, and none has been more extensively counterfeited.' Genuine specimens of *Ninsei-yaki* are extremely rare, and when they do come into the market, native collectors stand ready to pay much more for them than the usual run of foreign travelers would.

"(b) SATSUMA-WARE, a beautifully decorated crackle ware, remarkable for its soft mellow tint and its rich gold and enamel ornamentations, known to most collectors as the most valuable faience in E. Asia, is now often referred to as *Awata-yaki,* from the similarity of the wares and from the circumstance that some of the finest work is produced at the extensive pottery of *Sobei Kinkozan,* in the *Awata* district, at Kyoto. Its introduction in Japan is associated with the expedition to Korea of *Shimazu Yoshihisa, Daimyo* of Satsuma, who, on his return to his own country in 1598, brought with him a number of Korean potters, gave them the rank of *samurai,* and settled them in Kagoshima (in Satsuma Province) and at other places. The first generation of these immigrants manufactured only *Raku-yaki* (see p. ccliii.) In due time Kyoto took the lead in the manufacture of what is known to most Westerners as Satsuma-ware, and after *Nomura Ninsei* applied its decorative character to it, it became the principal ware of Kyoto. Several great names in the annals of the fictile arts were connected with the production of this ware during the 17th and 18th centuries, and several decorative styles were introduced and carried to remarkable perfection and refinement. The record of the present manufacturers commences with *Kagiya Tokuemon,* who began work at *Awata* in 1693. 'It was not till the time of *Kagiya Mohei,* the 3d generation, that the family acquired a wide reputation. This artist succeeded to his father's business, and in 1756 he had so distinguished himself as to be appointed potter to the *Tokugawa* Court in Yedo. In connection with this honor he received the name of *Kinkozan*[2], which he thenceforth stamped upon his best pieces, and which was similarly used by his successors. The manufactures of the present representative of the family have earned numerous medals and certificates at exhibitions at home and abroad. The *Kagiya* family carried the enameled decoration of Kyoto faience to its highest point of richness and brilliancy. Prior to their time the *Awata* glaze had been of a somewhat cold, hard character, but in their hands its color changed from grayish white to light buff, and it assumed an aspect of great delicacy and softness. To this warm, creamy ground a wealth of gold, red, green, and blue enamels was applied, the result being indescribably rich and mellow.'

"It is doubtful if any similar Japanese ware excels the

present-day Satsuma or *Awata-yaki* in decorative excellence. Many of the finest pieces vie with the old Satsuma-ware in delicacy of tone, and the mazy, crackled surface, coupled with the wonderful enamel effects secured by the pure gold and royal purple enrichments, appeal so strongly to porcelainists that few if any collections of importance lack one or more examples of what might be termed Japan's most national ware. It should be borne in mind, however, that despite the great number of pieces of so-called genuine old Satsuma sold each year in Japan, very few Western collections contain representative specimens. It has been pointed out that not more than a dozen pieces of legitimate old Satsuma have come into the market during the last 20 yrs., and that more than half of these have been bought in by native collectors at absurdly high prices. Few travelers, for instance, can distinguish the finest *Awata-yaki*, or even *Iwakura-yaki*, from real Satsuma. The ivory-like, lustrous glaze, and the almost microscopic crackle of the early pieces are reproduced with extraordinary fidelity in the modern ware, as is the same red, green, purple, gold, black, yellow, and Prussian blue in the decorations. Should the practiced eye fail to differentiate the old from the new, it is a satisfaction to know that to the average Occidental, many of the modern pieces are more beautiful than the earlier ones. *Captain Brinkley* says that all the choice pieces potted prior to 1868 are small or of medium size, and that consequently all the large imposing examples included in many Western collections are of modern manufacture. As a rule the best pieces show a *pate* with a grain almost as hard as porcelain biscuit, while the imitations, albeit they may bear chaste and beautiful decorations, are usually made of a chalky, porous *pate*. In the latter the crackle (which is produced intentionally), instead of being fine and hairlike, has rather the appearance of fissures — and in this it resembles the older Chinese *craquelé* faience. The Japanese call this crackled clay ware *Hibi-yaki*, and they employ in its manufacture a glaze of feldspar with leached wood ashes, which assimilate with the glazing material, making it more easily fusible.

"Usually there is a noteworthy difference in the Satsuma manufactured for export and that for the home market. Japanese connoisseurs will not buy the former, and the traveler will generally get better value for his money in buying such pieces as carry ornamentation liked by the natives. One will generally find, in examining an object painted for the foreign market, that however much labor has been bestowed on the body of the piece, the less prominent portions are somewhat defective, and whereas lusterless pigments predominate on certain of the modern examples, the decoration of the old and of the finest work consists of pure, jewel-like enamels. So much of this decoration is so exquisitely fine and complicated that it has to be done with a powerful magnifying glass, and casual buyers neither see nor look for imperfections. The more intricate the decoration, the greater the accuracy of execution, and the more skillful the use of the proper enamels, the higher is the price demanded for a piece. 'Evidences of age in a piece of Satsuma-ware are of all things the most deceptive, and any piece which has the cracks filled with what at first blush might suggest the accumulated dust of years should be rejected. Trituration with dirt, steeping in strong infusions of tea, exposure to the fumes of damp incense, boiling in decoctions containing sulphuric acid, etc., are methods not unusually employed by untrustworthy dealers. In some districts, notably in Owari, counterfeit Satsuma is made openly, and the perpetrators of the fraud do not hesitate to adopt any plan to make the deception more complete. Medicated and begrimed specimens of this ware are successfully palmed off on unsuspecting foreigners to an incredible extent, and will probably continue to find purchasers so long as men are sanguine enough to fancy that the long-since depleted curio-market still contains treasures accessible to themselves alone, and so long as the disfigurements of age and the blemishes of wear find people who regard them as beauties. The decoration of some of these pieces is so coarse that it does not assort ill with patches of grime and stains of lye added to simulate antiquity.' (*Brinkley*.)

"(c) THE KIYOMIZU-WARE, under which term wares other than those produced at *Awata, Iwakura,* and *Mizoro* are classed, comprises many beautiful examples of ceramic art. The first recorded potter of *Kiyomizu* faience was *Seibei Yahyo*, who established himself at *Gojo-zaka* about 1690, and whose pottery was moved to the *Koyomizu* district between 1781 and 1788. Here, at a later date, the first porcelain ever produced in Kyoto was made. The scores of kilns, which now stud the district, produce such a variety of wares that a book would be needed to catalogue them. Here the traveler will find attractive blue-and-white porcelains in an infinity of shapes; lovely celadon ware; pieces with beautiful aubergine, turquoise, yellow, coral, and other glazes; innumerable conceits of shape and varieties of faience, and of glazed and unglazed pottery, and a choice in dainty native teapots which no other place can offer. Beside the local wares, those from other provinces, and even from distant China, are copied and sold as originals. Much of the porcelain for export is made here, and most of it is moderate in price.

"(d) KUTANI-WARE (or Kaga porcelain) ranks high among the ceramic productions of Japan, and the best pieces, because of their careful, effective, and peculiar decoration, are classed by some with the most beautiful that the industry has furnished. It is believed to owe its origin to *Maeda Toshiharu*, feudal lord of *Daishoji*, in Kaga Province, who, after coming into power in 1639, brought a potter from Kyoto and commissioned him to seek material for fine clay wares. A bed of excellent porcelain stone was soon discovered near the village of *Kutani*, and the ceramic industry was inaugurated. It did not, however, become of much importance until the secrets of the Arita potters had been filched from them by one *Goto Saijiro*, who went to Hizen for the purpose.

Upon his return in 1664, the *Kutani* potters rapidly attained a high standard of skill. 'The wares that they produced (says *Captain Brinkley*) were of two kinds. The first, and more characteristic, was *Ao-Kutani*, so called from a deep-green (*ao*) glaze, of great brilliancy and beauty, which was largely used in its decoration. This glaze (along with yellow, purple, and soft Prussian blue) was applied so as to form diapers, scrolls, and floral designs, or was simply run over patterns traced in black on the biscuit. The chief colors used in the second class were green and red, supplemented by purple, yellow, blue (enamel), silver, and gold. The *Kutani* red was a specialty, — a peculiarly soft, subdued, opaque color, varying from rich Indian red to russet brown. For designs the early potters copied miniature landscapes, flowers ruffled by the breeze, sparrows perched among plum branches, and other glimpses of nature in her simplest garb. On some of their choice pieces the decoration is of a purely formal character, — diapers, scrolls, and medallions inclosing conventional symbols. On others it is essentially pictorial. The amateur may be tolerably confident that specimens decorated with peacocks, masses of chrysanthemums and peonies, figures of wrinkled saints, brightly appareled ladies, cocks upon drums, etc., belong to the manufactures of modern times. For decorative effect, combined with softness and artistic beauty, the *Ao-Kutani* has, perhaps, no equal. Its charm is due primarily to the admirable harmony of its colors and to their skillful massings; and secondarily to the technical excellence shown in the manner of applying the enamels.'

"The *Kutani-ware*, exported so largely, usually carries decorations of red and gold, with human figures, flowers, birds, clouds, etc. 'The execution is often of a very high character, — miniature painting which for delicacy and accuracy leaves nothing to be desired. Especially is this true of pieces having a multitude of tiny figures in gold depicted with microscopic fidelity on a solid red ground.' This flashy modern ware is not so pleasing to the educated foreign taste, and is incomparably less rich than the older *Ao-Kutani*. The early *Kutani* potters did not use their names to mark pieces, but put the factory name (*Kutani*) or employed the ideograph *fuku* ('good fortune'). The use of names (which are of the decorators, and not the potters) does not date farther back than 1850. Several other wares of considerable beauty are made in Kaga Province, under the name *Kaga-yaki*."

Other passages I found useful to Nippon collectors follow:

"Porcelain. Shops for the sale of cheap porcelain are scattered all over the city (fine wares at *Arthur & Bond's* and other places), but as the cost of transportation home on cheap ware is the same as on the finest, the latter is usually the most satisfactory to buy. The *Makuzu Kozan* kilns where the *Makuzu* porcelain (one of the most famous of the Japanese wares) is made, lie in the N. W. suburb (1631 Minamiotamachi) of Yokohama, in the Ota-mura district (2 M. from the *Grand Hotel*; jinriki, 30 *sen*) and should be visited by whosoever is interested in one of Japan's finest arts. The traveler is shown the workshops where the potters sit at their primitive wheels fashioning the clay into shape; the rooms where the decorations are added; the kilns where the pieces are fired; and extensive showrooms where many beautiful specimens of the ware (no two alike) are exhibited. Visitors are welcome whether or not they buy; the fixed prices are marked in plain figures; and considering the rare beauty of the objects, and the fame of the potter, are conspicuously moderate.

"The original factory was established in Kyoto in a district known as *Makuzu-ga-hara*, from which circumstance the pottery (transferred to Yokohama in 1871) derived its name. The original artist, *Miyagawa Kozan* (son of the celebrated Kyoto potter *Chobei*, who worked at Gion and produced a faience known to porcelainists as *Makuzu-yaki*), is a member of the Board of Imperial Household Artist, and with his son, *Miyagawa Hanzan*, is ranked as one of the finest ceramists that Japan has produced. The products of the factory are porcelains proper, and the pieces suggest in their delicate beauty the monochromes and polychromes of the Chinese *Kang-hsi* and *Yung-cheng* kilns. Jars, vases, bowls, plaques, quaint teapots, and a variety of beautiful objects skillfully decorated with flowers, bamboos, or other designs, in harmonious tints that show just beneath the glaze, are his specialties. Along with these are produced some of the finest blue-and-white pieces the collector will meet with in Japan. Equally famous are his apple-green glazes, so admired by American collectors. To *Kozan (or Shozan) Mr. Brinkley (Oriental Series,* vol. 8, p. 418) gives the credit of having inaugurated Chinese fashions in Japan, and to have set other Japanese artists to reproducing in Japan copies of the Chinese masterpieces. *Kozan's* best work ranks with choice *Kang-hsi* specimens. — Travelers will do well to have their purchases (for foreign shipment), packed at the pottery (where great care is given them), then delivered to the shipping-agent."

"Arita, a small town in a valley between hills aptly exemplifies the phrase, *Hic natus ubique notus,* for the name is known wherever porcelainists foregather. Here, and at *Imari*, the widely popular *Arita-yaki* is made in crude potteries small in comparison with their output and their fame. The station platform is usually piled high with cylindrical, straw-wrapped bundles awaiting shipment to the curio centers of Japan and abroad.

"According to *Dr. Rein* the manufacture of Porcelain at Arita is generally traced to *Gorodayu Shonsui*, a potter of *Ise* Province, who lived at the beginning of the 16th cent., and was the first in Japan to manufacture porcelain proper as distinguished from pottery. Moved by the beauty and value of Chinese porcelain, which began to reach Japan at this time, he undertook a journey to *King-te-tschin* via *Fuchow*, and remained there 5 yrs. to learn the trade. Returning in 1514 he settled in the then insignificant town of *Arita* and prepared from the materials he had brought from China a number of coarse porcelain wares decorated under glaze with blue cobalt. When his stock of Chinese porcelain material was exhausted, and he found himself obliged to depend on domestic clay, he could make nothing but faience, as did his successors to the end of the century, with cobalt decorations under glaze. Ceramics received a new impulse here (and in many other parts of Japan) with the return of *Hideyoshi's* army from Korea (in 1598). *Nabe-shima Naoshige,* the *daimyo* of *Hizen* Province, and one of the commanders of the Japanese troops in Korea, brought back with him several Korean potters, who settled first in the bathing-resort of *Ureshimo,* but later in *Arita.* One of them, *Risampei,* discovered, in 1599, porcelain stone on the *Idzumi-yama* E. of *Arita,* and at once began the manufacture of porcelain in Japan. The use of red oxide of iron followed some yrs. after that of cobalt decoration under glaze (thought by some to have been brought out by the Dutch), and 2 yrs. later decoration on glaze was introduced by *Higashijima Tokuemon* and *Sakaida Kakiemon,* potters, of *Arita,* who learned the process from the captain of a Chinese junk, at *Nagasaki.* The Dutch, as early as 1680, imported 'Old Hizen' from *Nagasaki,* and all the porcelain brought into Europe previous to 1854 by them is known as *Arita, Imari,* or *Hizen* ware — the first name denoting the place of manufacture; the 2d, the neighboring shipping-port; the 3d, the province in which the two, together with *Nagasaki,* are situated. — For many yrs. the *Arita* industry was the most highly developed and the most conspicuous of all the Japanese potteries. The range of hills lying to the E. furnished inexhaustible quantities of porcelain stone of incomparable quality — a peculiar material from which pottery of the most varying forms is made, from the light and finest eggshell porcelain to the imposing vases 6 or more ft. high. It is a product of the transformation of the old volcanic rock which is found close by in an unchanged state as perlite breccia and trachyte (a compact rock with 2.5-2.7 specific gravity). Its color is a grayish white or soft yellow, resembling trachyte or felsite clay-stone. The best kind is almost pure kaolin, while in other places the rock is conglomerate, and is intersected by numerous small quartz veins, partly filled with very small quartz crystals, and in other portions with crystals of iron pyrites, which under the microscope appear distinctly in the form of dice and pyritohedrons. There are 3 kinds of this quarried porcelain stone: one white and entirely kaolinized, which also possesses the earthy character of Kaolin; one blue and rich in quartz; and a third yellow, and containing iron.

"For centuries *Arita* furnished the most highly valued wares of Japan, its porcelain was perfectly uniform, and besides adding considerable translucence to pure white, was hard enough for all the purposes of ordinary life. It burns so easily that decorative art has in its surface, as in that of faience, a fine field, and is aided also by the plastic character of the excellent material. The earlier pieces were chiefly large, urn-shaped, covered jars, or *tsubo* (a contraction of *tsubogane*), called tea-urns because they served originally for preserving tea; also of hemispherical dishes or deep bowls (*domburi*), and round, flat plates (*sara*). They were decorated with peonies and chrysanthemums, small landscapes, human figures in red and gold, with sometimes a little green. The use of blue, violet, yellow, and black muffle colors belongs to a later period. Certain of *Kakiemon's* early masterpieces were of milk-white porcelain, generally with scanty designs in vitrifiable enamels. These delicate designs were too tame for the Dutch traders, who suggested that the potters should add enamel decoration over the glaze to pieces already decorated with blue under the glaze. 'There thus came into existence' (says *Brinkley*) 'the familiar *Imari-yaki;* the 'Old Japan' of Western amateurs; the *Nishiki-de* or 'Brocade Pattern' of the Japanese themselves. It was a brilliant ware, depending chiefly upon wealth of decoration and richness of coloring. Now nothing is rarer in enamel *Imari* porcelain than a good blue, and nothing is commoner than a specimen in which the decoration over the glaze gives evidence of great care and skill, while the blue designs under the glaze are blurred or of impure tone. In brilliancy, purity, variety, and accuracy of application, the enamels of the choice *Imari* specimens have never been surpassed. They were always painted with extreme care, their blue under glaze rich and clear, their red soft, uniform, and solid. Ranking first among the enamels found on the finest pieces is purple, a peculiar amethystine tinge, verging upon lilac. Then comes opaque yet lustrous green, the color of young onion sprouts, — beautiful enamel, much prized by the Japanese, who call it *tampan* (sulphate of copper). Then follows turquoise blue, and finally black, the first, however, being exceptional. Add to these red, grass-green, gold and blue (*sous couverte*), and the palette alike of the *Arita* and *Nabeshima* ceramists is exhausted. In old pieces of *Imari both enameled and blue-and-white* cracquelé is sometimes found. The *cracquelé* celadon, of which quantities now appear in the market under the name of *Hizen-yaki,* is a recent manufacture.'

"The same authority warns collectors against elaborately modeled and highly decorated specimens of *Imari* porcelain which are placed upon the market by unprincipled dealers as examples of *Kakiemon's* work. There were several generations of *Kakiemons,* and the mere fact of ascribing a specimen to *Kakiemon* is sufficient to proclaim the ignorance or dishonesty of the description. As for the figures of richly robed females that have received this title in recent works on Japanese art, they are manifest forgeries. 'Exquisite specimens of enameled ware were produced at the *Arita* factories, but the workmen generally adhered to a custom handed down from the days of *Tokuemon* and *Kakiemon,* — instead of making their vases with their own names or those of the year periods, they either copied Chinese seals and dates, or used a conventional ideograph or group of ideographs, quite useless for purposes of identification. The amateur is, therefore, without any easy guide to determine the age or making of a piece. He must look only to the quality of the *pate*, the brilliancy of the enamels, and the purity and intensity of the blue under the glaze. Any appearance of chalkiness in the clay indicates youth, and, as a general rule, the clearer and more metallic the ring of the biscuit, the greater the age of the piece. The color of the blue under the glaze is also a help. The tone is richest and most pleasing in specimens manufactured during the 18th cent.; in vases of earlier date it is often impure and blurred. To very choice, elaborate, and carefully finished examples of enameling it will generally be unsafe to assign a greater age than 150 yrs., and from what has been stated above, the amateur will see that the colors of the enamels afford some slight assistance: the red should be deep and even, with a dull, rather than a glossy surface; while lemon-yellow, purple, and black in combination are evidences at once of choice ware and of middle-period (1700-1830) manufacture. In the wares of the *Kakiemon* school there is found a cream-white surface sometimes almost equal to the ivory-white of Korea and China, and this color of the biscuit is another easily detected point. But specimens of this sort belong to the *Nabeshima-yaki*, rather than to genuine *Imari-yaki*. The biscuit of the latter, also, ought to be white, — the whiter the better, — but a perfectly pure white is seldom, if ever, found. This, however, may be said: that a surface showing a marked tinge of blue is not of fine quality, and that the more pronounced the tinge the less valuable the specimen. Examined attentively, the glaze of *Imari-yaki* presents the apperance of very fine muslin. It is pitted all over with microscopic points, which become more and more distinct as a later and less careful period of manufacture is approached. Spur-marks, 3 or 5 in number, the remains of little clay pillars upon which the specimen was supported in the furnace, are frequently found on the bottom of plates and other flat objects, something never seen on Chinese porcelain.'

"Westward from *Arita* the rly. traverses a semi-tropical region to 114 M. *Mikawachi*, known likewise for its potteries.

"Few Japanese wares are better known to foreign collectors than the Eggshell Porcelain (*Usu-de-yaki*, or 'thin-burned' ware) made here, but attributed to the *Arita* factories and called *Hizen*-ware. The best, most finely pulverized and purified material is used in its manufacture. The dishes and cups are turned quite thin on a sharpened wooden gauging-rod, then left upon it several days to dry in the open air, when, like the pieces of vases, they are further turned on the wheel, though much more thoroughly, and again burned in cases. There are two chief varieties, both of great fineness and purity, and both of gossamer-like consistency. One is decorated with blue under the glaze; the other with red, gold, and sometimes light blue above the glaze. Figure subjects — warriors in armor or courtezans in elaborate drapery — constitute the general decoration, which is seldom executed with any conspicuous skill. The date of its first production cannot be fixed with absolute accuracy, but authorities believe that it was not manufactured before the latter part of the 18th cent. A pretty conception in the ware made for export was to protect the more fragile wine-cups by envelopes of extraordinarily fine plaited basket-work (*ajiro-gumi*) made in *Nagasaki* — whither the cups were sent for sale, usually in nests of 3, 5, or 7."

"Cloisonné Enamel (*shippo*), though long known to the Chinese, is thought to have gained its first foothold in Japan near the close of the 16th cent., when *Hirata Hokoshiro* established himself at Nagoya and began the manufacture, in a small way, of various decorative articles. The name *shippo* (or *jippo*) means the 'seven precious things,' — gold, silver, lapis-lazuli, coral, agate, rock-crystal, and pearl, — and was no doubt applied by the Japanese to vari-colored enamel-encrusted wares because of the ancient custom (practiced in Constantinople, Egypt, China, and elsewhere) of decorating gold, silver, and copper vessels with precious and semi-precious stones. Of the two prominent processes, pit or embedded enamel (*champlevé*), and the cell or encrusted enamel (*cloisonné*), the latter is the most popular among the Japanese; the cells or *cloisons* are formed separately of narrow metal bands corresponding to the pattern of the decoration, and then soldered to the foundation. This process of enamel decoration requires considerable technical skill and is essentially as follows: —

"After the object to be decorated has been fashioned in thin copper (or silver), the decorations are sketched or traced on its surface, generally after patterns, with white-lead varnish or India ink. The *cloisons* are formed by means of narrow strips of gold, silver, or copper delicately graded, heated beforehand to take out the elasticity, curved into the required shape with a pair of wire pincers, and first cemented, then soldered to the surface. When in this position, standing on their edges, they outline the design and form-inclosing spaces, to receive the enamel pastes. These are now packed in, color after color, and when the cells are filled the object is placed in an oven and subjected to a heat sufficient to vitrify the pastes without affecting the metals forming the base and the cells. The colors shrink considerably under the application of heat, and holes are formed in the enamel, so that there must be a continual filling-up of the *cloisons*. The vessel is subjected to a second firing, then rubbed and polished. The cracks and other hollows in the cells are again filled up and improved, then burnt for the third time, and often a fourth, and once more rubbed and polished. After the vitrified pastes have completely filled the spaces, the whole surface is ground and polished with varying grades of soft stone and with great care until it becomes perfectly even and shows a soft luster. Pieces finished in this manner are called *kazari-jippo*, or ornamental enamel. When translucid pastes are employed, the grinding and polishing are often dispensed with. The greatest care is given to fine pieces by reputable dealers. Imitations are often made by subjecting the object to one or two firings, then filling in the holes and cracks with vegetable tallow, rather than take the time to fill in and burn the piece properly. The more intricate the design, the softer the color; the finer the wire, and the higher the finish, the more costly is the article. Kyoto and Nagoya are headquarters for the manufacture not only of articles of some merit, but also of many deceitful imitations. Here also are made some of the handsome monochrome enamels — yellow, red, aubergine purple, grass-green, dove-gray, lapis-lazuli, etc. Very charming effects are produced in some of this work by spreading translucid enamels over chiseled or decorated bases that show through the diaphanous covering. A gold or a silver base deeply chiseled in wave-diaper, and overrun with a paste of aubergine purple, is a popular design, as is also one showing a brilliant little gold-fish swimming through a medium of tender blue heightened by a background of shimmering silver.

"The highly artistic work of *Namikawa Sosuke*, of Tokyo, stands practically in a class apart from the *cloisonné* enamel, and is known as *Musen-jippo*, or *cloison*-less enamel. In this work, which came into prominence about 1880 and which has been brought to a high degree of perfection by the inventor, *Namikawa Sosuke*, and his son, beautiful and imperishable pictures in vitrified pastes are produced, 'remarkable as to technical skill, harmonious and at the same time rich in coloring, and possessing pictorial qualities which could not reasonably have been looked for in such material. There is nothing like them to be found in any other country, and they stand at an immeasurable distance above the ordinary *cloisonné* creations. The design, which is usually placed in a monochromatic field of low tone, is framed, at the outset, with a ribbon of thin metal, after the manner of ordinary *cloisonné*-ware; but as the work proceeds, the *cloisons* are hidden, — unless their presence would contribute to give necessary emphasis to the design, — and the final result is a picture in vitrified enamel.' Vases, panels, bowls, flat pictures several ft. sq., depicting fowls, animals, land- and sea-scapes, flowers, and a wide variety of subjects, are to be found in this uniquely beautiful work in an almost endless scale of shades and tones. Not a few of the motifs are the most famous paintings of the early masters, which are copies in enamel with a fidelity to the originals that is extraordinary. In reproducing some of the old pictures, the *cloisons* are hidden or omitted, or freely used, and the reproductions are so minute and so faithful that the particular shades of antiquity belonging to the silk or paper on which the picture was originally painted appear on the copies. The intricate and tedious process of painting the enamels on, then the firing and polishing, can be seen by travelers at *Mr. Namikawa's* studio (English spoken) at 8, *Shinyemon-cho, Nihonbashi-ku*, Tokyo. Here, too, are made many of the beautiful gold-enameled decorations used by the Imperial Japanese Gov't. — A *cloisonné* shop in *Shippoya*."

From *Terry's Guide to Japanese Empire* by Thomas. P. Terry

From the National Archives, Record Group No. 59, Report No. 532, dated May 26, 1881, report from Consul-General Thomas B. Van Buren to John Hay, Assistant Secretary of State. Subject: Visit and address from the officials of the Aichi-Ken and the village of Seto in the porcelain district:

"To the Honorable John Hay, Assistant Secretary of State, Washington.

"Sir:

"A few days since I was waited upon by two officials of the Kencho (government office) of Aichi-Ken, the province in which the city of Nagoya is situated, and the Kocho, or village officer of Seto, where the manufacture of porcelain is carried on; and the latter presented me an address, which, translated, reads as follows:

" 'Sir:

" 'After the Seto porcelain received awards in each of the exhibitions of France, America and Australia, the demand for it has increased, and, accordingly, the number of pieces manufactured has also increased, so that the value of manufacture at Seto amounted in a year to 300,000 yen. In 1880, however, it was reduced to 200,000 yen which is due to the very high price of fuel, etc., for which reason it could not be sold as cheaply. The fact that, to manufacture the porcelain consumed considerable time and that the paintings were poor, perhaps, were also additional causes for the falling off of the receipts.

" 'On the 10th of November last, you, with General Le Gendre and Dr. Latham, had the kindness to visit Seto village, and you delivered an address in which you suggested certain improvements in the manufacture of porcelain. On the 21st of the same month, Mr. Utsunouriya Goudaigicho came and also kindly made an address to the same effect - that the ovens should be improved, etc. From that time, some of the manufacturers have comprehended that the oven improvements and right methods of manufacture must necessarily be made, and in February of this year, they did improve the ovens and tried and understood the convenience. Kato Kaushiro and four others consulted as to the making the manufacture of porcelain as cheap as possible and to see that the Seto article should take a prominent position among exported products. Mr. Kato and the others received an order from a merchant to manufacture several thousands of small vases. These men did not listen to timid suggestions, not caring how much money they expended in valuable experiments, and they diligently engaged themselves in seeking the best methods of manufacture and in discovering a way of using less fuel, and thus preventing great waste and setting an example before the other manufacturers. On the 7th of March, 1881, Mr. Kato arrived at a very satisfactory result. Before this, some manufacturers doubted whether the experiments would be successful, because they were acquainted only with small and incomplete ovens, which would not produce perfect and uniform sets, while the baking required a long time and much fuel. But, during these experiments, hundreds of people thronged to see them, even late into the night.

" 'This is owing to your kind suggestions, which incited the ambition of these gentlemen and awakened the manufacturers from their dream. Estimating the expense of fuel for a year to be 80,000 yen, the improvement of ovens only has reduced it to 60,000 yen. Moreover, when good roads are made to give convenience for transportation, the danger of the porcelain from breaking will be lessened. Such is the present condition as regards improvements that have been made in all the ovens. The methods of manufacture and decoration will be improved in a few months. It is a source of great happiness, not only to Seto village, but to our whole country, to see that Seto porcelain is likely to take so prominent a position among our exports.

(Sgd.) Sano Mastatsu
      Seto Mura Kocho
      Aichi Ken

May 1881'

"The Ken officials then presented me, on behalf of the governor of the Ken, with a pair of beautiful vases, as a testimonial of the estimation in which my remarks to the proprietors of the porcelain works at Seto, on my late visit there, were held by the officials and manufacturers of the Ken. I had the pleasure of entertaining the gentlemen at dinner, and we parted with mutual expressions of respect.

(Sgd) Thomas Van Buren
      Consul-General"

NOTE: In 1880, Van Buren states that one yen equals $0.997, or approximately $1.00 in U.S. gold dollars.

" 'Fine Japanese Ware', (author unknown), August 6, 1881, *New York Times*:

"Consul-General Van Buren's report on the pottery and porcelain industries of Japan is an able resumé of the knowledge we at present possess on the subject, and contains at the same time much that is both original and interesting. The writer justly dwells on the very great natural advantages Japan enjoys in the matter of ceramic manufacture. The potter has only to dig. Excellent porcelain clays are found everywhere, and often near 'water transportation'. No doubt much of Japan's success as a porcelain producing country is attributable to this cause. We know that in China the discovery of real fine pure clay was regarded as the result of divine intervention, and the memory of the 'inspired', who

showed the people where they might find 'boccaro' earth is gratefully remembered to this day. In Europe, too, those who have studied the subject are familiar with the troubles that beset the potter of the Boboli gardens and the family of the Chiccanean. Nevertheless, to the artificial clay of those times we owe the exquisite pate tendre of the old Sevres ware; a bisquit so much superior in many respects to that obtained from the natural kaolin, that 45 years after the latter had come into general use, a neglected store of the artificial material made the fortune of its finder, Ebelman. It is not a mere freak that induces people to give 500 guineas for a saucer of old Sevres.

"But even in Japan certain districts are more favored by nature than others. The Comparative table which the Consul-General gives is most interesting in this respect, for it shows how largely local advantages have influenced the development of the ceramic art in the various Provinces. Mikawa, now better known as Aichi-ken, stands first on the list, but much of the clay found there is not of the best quality. Hizen, as might be expected, comes next, and after it Mino, where the best egg-shell porcelain in Japan has been manufactured; a fact which the author, we observe, does not note. Kaga finds no place on the list at all, and this may perhaps surprise the very numerous lovers of that brilliant red and gold ware so largely exported to Europe at present. But the fact is that, despite the celebrity of the Kutanyaki, the Province of Kashiu possesses neither kaolin nor petunse of first class quality. The potters of Daishoji have always been obliged to import their materials, and hence it happens that the amateur is often sadly puzzled by the specimen decorated after the Kutani style, but made of Hizen or Owari clay.

"Apropos of this Kagayaki, the author seems inclined to agree with the idea that it is the representative of the 'graphic style' in Japan. No doubt this dictum is true at present, but it is well to remember that delineation of 'trades, occupations, sports, customs and costumes' are never found on the Kutani ware of former times. Something similar may be said of the nature of the ware. the Consul-General describes it as faience, which is true of the Kagayaki proper, i.e. the ware made entirely with materials found in the Province, but the best pieces produced there in the past, and indeed much of the workshops' present outcome, must be described as fine porcelain."

In 1903, William Griffis wrote the book *The Mikado's Empire*. In his chapter entitled "The Mythical Zoology of Japan," he describes the Japanese dragon (tatsu) as the only animal in modern Japan that wears hairy ornaments on the upper lip. He says the creature looks like a winged crocodile except as to the snout which is tufted with hair, and the claws, which are very sharp. The Japanese author, Baken, when writing *Hakkenden* (*The Eight Dog Children*) describes the monster in the following way: "The dragon is a creature of a very superior order of being. It has a deer's horns, a horse's head, eyes like those of a devil, a neck like that of a snake, a belly like that of a red worm, scales like those of a fish, claws like a hawk's, paws like a tiger's, and ears like a cow's. In the spring, the dragon lives in heaven; in the autumn, in the water; in the summer, it travels in the clouds and takes its pleasure; in winter, it lives in the earth dormant. It always dwells alone, and never in herds. There are many kinds of dragons, such as the violet, the yellow, the green, the red, the white, the black, and the flying dragon. Some are scaly, some horned, some without horns. When the white dragon breathes, the breath of its lungs goes into the earth and turns to gold. When the violet dragon spits, the spittle becomes balls of pure crystal, of which gems and caskets are made. One kind of dragon has nine colors on its body, and another can see everything within a hundred ri; another has immense treasures of every sort; another delights to kill human beings. The water dragon causes floods of rain; when it is sick, the rain has a fishy smell. The fire dragon is only seven feet long, but its body is of flame. The dragons are all very lustful, and approach beasts of every sort. The fruit of a union of one of these monsters with a cow is the kirin; with a swine, an elephant; and with a mare, a steed of the finest breed. The female dragon produces at every parturition nine young. The first young dragon sings, and likes all harmonious sounds, hence the tops of Japanese bells are cast in the form of this dragon; the second delights in the sounds of musical instruments, hence the koto, or horizontal harp, and suzumi, a girl's drum struck by the fingers, are ornamented with the figure of this dragon; the third is fond of drinking, and likes all stimulating liquors, therefore goblets and drinking cups are adorned with representations of this creature; the fourth likes steep and dangerous places, hence gables, towers, and projecting beams of temples and pagodas have carved images of this dragon upon them; the fifth is a great destroyer of living things, fond of killing and bloodshed, therefore swords are decorated with golden figures of this dragon; the sixth loves learning and delights in literature, hence on the covers and title-pages of books and literary works are pictures of this creature; the seventh is renowned for its power of hearing; the eighth enjoys sitting, hence the easy-chairs are carved in its images; the ninth loves to bear weight, therefore the feet of tables and of hibachi are shaped like this creature's feet. As the dragon is the most powerful animal in existence, so the garments of the emperor or mikado are called the 'dragon robes,' the ruffling of the 'dragon scales' his displeasure, and his anger the 'dragon wrath.' "

William Griffis describes another creature in his book and says that its visits are rarer than those of angels, since it appears on the earth only at millennial intervals, or at the birth of some very great man. "This fabulous bird, also of Chinese origin, is called the howo, or phenix (sic). The tombs of the shoguns at Shiba and Nikko have most elaborate representations of the howo, and the new and old paper currency of the country bears its image. It seems to be a combination of the pheasant and peacock. A Chinese dictionary thus describes the fowl: 'The phenix is of the essence of water; it was born in the vermillion cave; it roosts not but upon the most beautiful tree; it eats not but of the seeds of the bamboo; it drinks not but of the sweetest spring; its body is adorned with the Five colors; its song contains the Five Notes; as it walks, it looks around; as it flies, the hosts of birds follow it.' It has the head of a fowl, the crest of a swallow, the neck of a snake, the tail of a fish. Virtue, obedience, justice, fidelity, and benevolence are symbolized in the decorations on its head, wings, body, and breast."

Other creatures described by Griffis are the kappa, the kama-itachi, the "thunder-god", the jishin uwo, tengu and shojo. The kappa is a creature with the body and head of a monkey and the claws of a tortoise. The kama-itachi is believed to be a type of weasel. This mythical animal cuts or tears the faces of people with the sickle which it is supposed to carry. Griffis tells us that the "thunder-god" is represented as a creature that looks like a human dwarf changed into a semicircle of five drums joined together. When he strikes or rattles these drums he makes thunder. The jishin uwo is also called the "earthquake fish." "This fish strikes the shore or ocean bottom in its gambols or in its wrath, and makes the ground rock and tremble. The tengu is a long billed goblin that haunts mountain places and kidnaps wicked children and the shojo is a Japanese bacchanal. They live near the sea, have long red hair, bleared eyes and gaunt faces and dance with wild joy before a large jar of sake."

---

[1]The word PORCELAIN is derived from *porcellana*, a name given to the ware by the Portuguese traders under the belief that it was made from the fusion of eggshells and fish's glue and scales to resemble the beautifully polished, nacreous surface of the Venus-shell (*Cypræda*) — the curved shape of the upper surface of which resembles the curve of a pig's back (*porcella*, a little pig; diminutive of *porco*; fem. *porca*). A porcelain shop is *Tsuchi-yakiya* (or *Setomonoya*; or *Zikiya*, etc., depending upon the class of ware sold).

[2]The *Kinkozan* Pottery with its 77 kilns is perhaps one of the best places for the traveler interested in the subject to study the process of manufacture and decoration. The showrooms (English spoken) contain a superb collection of modern wares and a few ancient speciments of interest to antiquarians. The clay employed in making the ware comes from *Shigaraki*, in *Omi* Province.

OLD ADS FOR NIPPON CHINA

JAPANESE CHINA CUPS AND SAUCERS.
Transparent China.

L1551 — 3½ x 2, saucer 5 in., ovide, allover Japanese figure and landscape, Tokio red handle and edge. 1 doz. in pkg. **Doz. 95c**

L1550—3¾x2, saucer 5½, allover blue print decorations. 1 doz. in pkg. ....**Doz. $1.15**

◆◆◆◆ A LEADER. ◆◆◆◆
Try it out this season.

L1553 — 3¾x2, saucer 5½, selected, allover girls and tea garden, gold and Tokio red edge. **Matches plate.** **L1628** 1 doz. in pkg. Doz. **$1.25**

L1549 — 3¾ x 2, saucer 5½, selected allover blue decoration. **Matches L1625 plate.** 1 doz. in pkg. **Doz. $1.25**

L6128 — 3¾x2, saucer 5½, 3 floral and foliage decorations with colored scroll, dark green, and maroon band edges, gold line handles. 1 doz. in pkg. asstd, **Doz. $1.35**

L6136 — 3¾x2, saucer 5½, 2 tone chrysanthemums, gold and green foliage, gold scroll ornamented cobalt blue edges and handle. 1 doz. in pkg ..**Doz. $1.50**

L6129 — 4¾x2, saucer 5½, characteristic allover Japanese figure and landscape enamel and gold traced Tokio red edges and handle. 1 doz. in pkg.............**Doz. $1.75**

L6567 — 3¾x2½, saucer 5½, fluted, pink and green bouquets, gold sprays and scroll border, gold striped edges, base and handle. 1 doz. in pkg.........**Doz. $1.80**

L6131—3¾x2, saucer 5½, Japanese decoration in colors, gold striped maroon panels alternating with floral bouquets in border, gold traced nile green edges. 1 doz. in pkg...... ......**Doz. $1.87**

L5015—3¾x2, saucer 5½, fluted inside decoration in colors and gold, gold traced Tokio red edges and handles, outer sprays. **Matches L6566 plate.** 1 doz. in pkg. **Doz. $1.95**

L6132—3⅞x2, saucer 5½, floral clusters with leaves, alternating with gold vines and flowers, gold ornamented cobalt blue edges and handle, spray inside. 1 doz. in pkg....**Doz. $2.00**

6138—3¾x2, saucer 5½, twin tinted floral and foliage medallions with gold sprays, embossed gold half circle divisions, ornamental green border, gold band edges and handle. **Matches L6273 plate.** 1 doz. in pkg...................**Doz. $2.20**

AFTER DINNER CUPS AND SAUCERS.

L1529 — 3x 1½, saucer 4¼, Mino china, allover pale green Japanese decorations. 1 doz. in pkg.......**Doz. Out**

◆◆◆◆◆ A LEADER. ◆◆◆◆◆
Direct importation at special price.

L1530—Cup 3x1⅞, saucer 4¼ in., Mino ware, all over blue decoration. 1 doz. in pkg. **Doz. 39c**

Butler Bros., Catalog #560, 1906

AFTER DINNER CUPS AND SAUCERS —Continued.

L1535—2⅞x1⅝, saucer 4¾ allover flowers and figures, red band edges. 1 doz. in pkg. **Doz. 84c**

L5004—2¾x2⅛, saucer 4¾, transparent china, allover Japanese floral and scenic decorations in natural colors. Tokio red band edge and handle. doz. in pkg. **Doz. 95c**

BREAD AND BUTTER PLATES.

L1617    L6265

L1617—6 in. fluted flange, Japanese girls and landscapes, colored floral borders, Tokio red edge. 1 doz. in pkg ....**Doz. 79c**
L6265—6 in. china, cobalt and gold edge, Japanese figure and landscape. 1 doz. in pkg. **Doz. 96c**

TABLE PLATES.

L1625—7½ in., blue and white, floral decoration, matches L1549 cup and saucer. 1 doz. in pkg. **Doz. $1.15**

⟋⟍ L6615 — ⟋⟍
Fancy design 8⅝ in., blue & white, growing iris and daisies, conventional border. 1 doz. in pkg. **$1.35**

L6566 — 7¼ in., fluted, Japanese figures and landscapes, natural colors with gold, gold traced Tokio red edges. ½ doz. in pkg. **Doz. $1.50**

L6272—7¼ in., transparent china, fluted flange, gold decorated scallop cobalt blue edge, 2 floral designs with profuse gold tracing. ½ doz. in pkg. asstd. **Doz. $1.85**

L6565 — 8½ in., transparent floral bouquet border, gold traced, floral center, gold vine cobalt edge. ½ doz. in pkg. **Doz. $2.10**

L6273 — 7¼ in., white china, twin tinted floral medallions, embossed gold framed ornamental green border, gold band edge. **Matches L6138 cup and saucer.** ½ doz. in pkg.....**Doz. $2.15**

L6276 — 8½ in., transparent china, twist fluted flange, colored Japanese landscape and mountain view with half framing of flowers, gold ornamented Tokio red edge. ½ doz. in pkg. ....**Doz. $2.15**

L6277 — 8½ in., thin china, gold illuminated temple, pagoda and landscape scenery, gold scroll traced cobalt blue edge. ½ doz. in pkg. **Doz. $2.25**

CHOCOLATE POTS.

L5110   L6281

L5110—Ht. 9½, convex paneled, gold decorated, Tokio red edges, handles and spout, decoration gold illuminated. 1 in pkg. **Each, 50c**

L6281—Ht. 9½, rib panel, allover enamel traced, colored floral sprays and gold vines, gold scroll wide cobalt edges and handle. 1 in pkg.................. ... ...**Each, 65c**

CONDENSED MILK JARS.

L6477    L6478

L6477—3¾x5, saucer 6¼, Japanese picture decorated, Tokio red edges, handles and knob. 3 in pkg...................**Each, 33c**

L6478—Ht. 5½ in., saucer 6 in., blue tinted surface, rose clusters sides and cover, gold beaded edges and ornamented handles and cover. 3 in pkg....................**Each, 39c**

SUGAR AND CREAM SET.

L6234—Sugar 4¼x3½, creamer 3¾x3, spiral ribbed, gold ornamented Kitani tea garden decoration, gold and maroon edges, handles and knobs. 3 sets in pkg............**Set, 50c**

EGG CUPS.

L5035   L5036   L5037

L5035 — 2 x 2½ in., blue Japanese figures. **Doz. 25c**

L5036—1¾x2½ in., allover figures and landscape, red edge. 1 doz. in pkg. **Doz. 32c**

L5037—2¾x3½, footed, allover picture decoration, Tokio red and gold edge ......**Doz. 75c**

INDIVIDUAL BUTTER PLATES.
1 doz. in pkg.

L1690   L1691    L1692

L1695

L1690—3¼ in. blue and white flowers...**Doz. 18c**
L1691—3¼ in., Tokio red edges, picture centers. **Doz. 24c**
L1692—3½ in., floral and gold wreath, gold edge. **Doz. 33c**
L1695—4½ in., Tokio red and blue edges, asstd, picture decoration. **Doz. 36c**

JAPANESE BREAD AND BUTTER PLATES.

1 doz. in pkg. unless specified.

L1615

L1619

L1615—6¼ in., fancy allover blue decorations of birds, dragons, floral and scroll designs. Doz. **72c**

L1619—6¼ in., shaded luster surface, floral and leaf decoration interwoven with gold, asstd. ....Doz. **$1.25**

L2233—6¼ in., deep fluted scallop cobalt blue edge gold decorated, allover floral cluster decoration with gold sprays. ½ doz. in pkg. Doz. **$1.50**

JAPANESE CHINA TABLE PLATES.

L1624—7½ in. diam., Mino ware, allover blue and white decorations, typical Japanese scene, heavy blue border around edges in lace effect. 1 doz. in pkg.....Doz. **$1.25**

L1919½—9 in., allover blue and white printed floral decoration. ½ doz. in pkg. Doz. **$1.35**

L1627—7½ in., decorated with Japanese figures, and scenes in colors, heavy red enameled band around edge. ½ doz. in pkg. Doz. **$1.50**

L1927½—7⅝ in., fluted sides, scalloped gold edge, hand painted gold trimmed decorations in enamel effects, outside decoration of birds in natural colors. ½ doz. in pkg...Doz. **$3.00**

L2250—8½ in., thin china, scallop fluted edge, allover Japanese landscape and figure decoration, floral border, Tokio red edge, profuse gold illuminations. 2 styles. ⅓ doz. in pkg..Doz. **$3.50**

JAPANESE CHINA CAKE PLATE.

L1835—10 in. coupe shape, dark green shaded luster ground with rich rose clusters, gold decorated with cobalt blue border, open handle, footed........ ....Each, **$1.25**

JAPANESE CHINA FANCY BONBON OR OLIVE DISH.

L2131—5½ in., fluted, Japanese girls, scene and floral decorations in Tokio red and colors with gold illuminations, red and gold scalloped border. ½ doz. in pkg. Doz. **$1.95**

JAPANESE CHINA BREAD AND MILK SET

L2100—6 in. plate, 4x2 bowl, 3½ in. cream pitcher, white china, hand painted Japanese figure and floral decoration, gold outlined, Tokio red edges, gold tracings. 3 sets in pkg. Doz. sets, **$3.50**

JAPANESE CHINA SALAD OR BERRY BOWLS.

L2088—Diam. 9½ in., profuse allover flower decorations in bright natural colors. Also 3 Japanese landscape decorations in medallion effect, heavy red enameled, gold traced border around edges. 1 in pkg...............Each, **65c**

L2087—Diam. 10 in., footed, melon shape, heavy gold scalloped edge, allover floral and gold spray decorations, beaded pink or green bands. 1 in pkg...Each, **75c**

JAPANESE CHINA SALT AND PEPPER SHAKERS.

6 salts and 6 peppers in pkg. of 1 doz. Opening in bottom.

L1730

L1736

L2176

L1737

L1730—2½, allover blue floral print decorations.................................Doz. **35c**

L1736—Chick shape, 2½ in., painted features and feet, natural color yellow shading, with painted wings..... .... Doz. **39c**

L2176—2¾x1¾, fancy hexagon shape, floral and gold spray decoration, gold clouded top. Doz. **39c**

L1737—Comical Japanese doll in sitting position, 2½ in., painted features, kimona in colors, enamel and gold decorated..Doz. **42c**

L2184—*Design and price are equally attractive.* Ht. 3¾ in., tapering column shape ribbed, floral decorated with gold tracings, wide gold decorated cobalt blue top and bottom edges.

Per dozen, **89c**

TOOTHPICK OR MATCH HOLDERS.

1 doz. in box unless stated.

L1738

L1739

L1506

L1738—1⅞x2⅛ in., allover blue decoration of floral and landscape scenes.......Doz. **32c**

L1739—2⅛ in., vase shape, asstd. hand painted Jap decorations of figures, landscapes and flowers, red band around neck, gold edge. Doz. **39c**

L1506—2¾ x 2⅛, panel pattern sides, rose and gold decoration on tinted luster ground, gold traced cobalt blue footed base and crimped top. ½ doz. in pkg.. ... .Doz. **96c**

JAPANESE CHINA CHOCOLATE POTS.

L2209

L2212

L2209—Ht. 7½ in., panel shape, gold traced fancy cobalt blue edges and handles, allover gold and colored floral spray decorations. ¼ doz. in pkg...............Doz. **$3.95**

L2213

L2212—9½ in., allover Japanese figure, landscape and water scenes profusely gold illuminated, green band edges, maroon handle and knob gold traced. 1 in pkg. Each, **75c**

L2213—9 in., fancy shape, ribbed, cream ground, rose cluster and embossed gold decoration, deep beaded gold top border, gold decorated handle and knob. 1 in pkg. Each, **90c**

JAPANESE CHINA CREAM PITCHER.

L1755—4 in., transparent china, fancy allover blue decoration, showing landscape, village and figures, blue trimmed handle. 1 doz. in pkg...............Doz. **85c**

JAPANESE CHINA ROSE BOWL.

L2077—3½x3½, cobalt blue feet and crimped edge gold decorated, roses and forget me nots with gold sprays. Asstd. decorations. ½ doz. pkg...Doz. **$2.10**

JAPANESE CHINA AFTER DINNER CUPS AND SAUCERS.

1 doz. in pkg. unless stated.

L2002—2x2, saucer 4, all over Japanese decoration, Tokio red and gold trimmed edge...Doz. **75c**

L2004—Cup 2½x2¼, saucer 4⅝, floral hand painted decorations, gold trimmings, asstd. blue, green and pink band edges, asstd. 6 decorations............Doz. **89c**

L2008—2¼x1¾, saucer 5 in., small fluted shape, allover hand painted Jap scenery decorations in rich colors and gold, Tokio red under gold edges and handle. ½ doz. in pkg. Doz. **$1.25**

L2011—2¼x3⅜, saucer 4½, new fancy shape, fluted, scalloped edge, tinted floral and gold decoration on shaded ground, gold traced fancy cobalt blue edges and handle. ½ doz. in pkg............Doz. **$1.75**

Butler Bros., catalog, 1908

JAPANESE CHINA TETE-A-TETE SETS.

Each set in box.

L2300—Tea pot 6 in., sugar 4½, creamer 3¾ in., cups 3x 1⅝, white china, allover Japanese figure and landscape decoration, Tokio red and gold edge, gold decorated handles. Set, 69c

L5230—Tea pot 4¼, sugar 3¾, creamer 3 in., 2 cups 3x2½, saucers 5 in., thin transparent china, floral and leaf decoration with gold filigree and scrolls, gold trimmed edges and handles.........................Set, ★90

L5231—Tea pot 5½, sugar 5, creamer 3¾ in., 2 cups 3x2, saucers 5 in., swell panel shape, Japanese Kitani decoration, maroon and gold edges, handle and spout.....Set, $1.50

L2302—Tea pot 6 x 4¼, sugar 5 x 3¾, creamer, 3¾ x 3, cups 3½ x 2¼, melon shape, gold cobalt blue feet, knob, handles and edges, floral and ornamental gold all around decoration, spray on outside of cups..Set, $1.75

L5232—Tea pot 6, sugar 5, creamer 4 in., 2 cups 2½x2¼, saucers 4¾ in., fine thin china, twisted grooved panel shape, elaborately enameled floral decoration, beaded ground, wide mosaic scroll border in gold and variegated colors, maroon gold traced edges, handles and spout.................Set, $1.95

JAPANESE CHINA HIGH CRACKER JARS.

L5236—5¾x6½, allover hand painted Japanese figure and floral Kitani decoration, Tokio red edges and knob. 2 in pkg.....Each, 36c

L5239—Ht. 5½ in., elaborate Japanese decorations with colored figures, hand painted flowers and oriental effects with heavy gold trimmings, lid with solid gold fancy flower handle. 2 in pkg.........Each, 57c

L5238—6 x 7½, white china allover Japanese figures and landscape decoration gold illuminated, gold decorated maroon and cobalt blue edges, foot and knob. 1 in pkg. Each, 75c

JAP CHINA LOW CRACKER JARS OR COVERED TABLE DISHES.

L5240—6x4, allover characteristic Japanese figure & landscape & floral decoration, gold illuminated gold traced Tokio red edges, handles & knob. 2 in pkg., asstd ...Each, 39c

L5241—6x4¼, allover floral leaf & gold filigree decoration, gold scroll traced scalloped cobalt edges, handles & knob. 1 in pkg. Each, 50c

L5243—7¼ x 4, ribbed, elaborate floral and leaf decoration, shaded luster ground, gold traced and heavily beaded scalloped edges, fancy handles and knob. 1 in pkg.................Each, $1.00

L5111—Ht. 9¼ in., ribbed panel shape, flaring base, gold outlined rose medallion and scroll floral spray decoration, gold traced cobalt edges, handle and spout. 1 in pkg. Each, 65c

L5112—Ht. 9¾ in., footed swell column shape, white china, allover delicately shaded crimson rose and leaf decoration with gold sprays, gold trimmed edges, handle and spout. 1 in pkg. Each, 78c

L5113—Ht. 9¼ in., swell panel shape, scattered rose and leaf cluster decoration on delicately clouded light color ground with vine scroll, fancy gold scroll border, gold handle and spout. 1 in pkg......Each, 95c

JAPANESE CHINA 3 PIECE SETS.

Some with Cups and Saucers to Match.

Good transparent china, hand painted decorations. Each set comprises tea pot, covered sugar bowl and cream pitcher. Each set in pkg.

L5100—Tea pot 5x4, sugar 4½x3½, creamer 4x3, ribbed melon shape, allover Japanese figure, flower and lantern decorations, gold outlined, Tokio red edges, handles, knobs and spout ....Set, 69c

L5103 — Tea pot 6, sugar 4½, creamer 4 in., fancy shape, embossed scalloped edges, fancy openwork handles, Tokio landscape decoration in delicate tints, narrow gold band edges and handles. Set, 89c

L5021—Cup 3⅝x2, saucer 5½ in., matches L5103........ Doz. $1.95

L5105—Tea pot 7, sugar 5½, creamer 4 in. fancy ribbed shape, green luster ground, natural color pansy & leaf decoration, gold & enameled traced, gold scroll & green and gold double borders, gold ornamented handles, knob & spout...................Set, $2.00

L5081—Sugar 4¾, creamer 3½ in. tapering panel shape, floral and leaf spray decoration gold traced, gold scroll cobalt band edges and handles. 3 sets in pkg...Per set, 33c

L5083—Sugar 4 in., creamer 3½ in., ribbed melon shape, floral and leaf spray enamel studded decoration gold decorated cobalt edges and fancy handles. 3 sets in pkg. Set, 36c

JAP CHINA MUSTARD POT.

L5039—3¾x3, dainty rose decorations with gold lace work, cobalt blue knob, side handles and edges, gold tracings. 1 doz. in pkg.......Doz. 96c

Butler Bros., Catalog #694, 1908

34

CUPS AND SAUCERS.

L5007 — Cup 3¾ x 2, saucer 5½, allover characteristic Japanese floral and landscape decoration. 1 dz.pkg......Doz. **89c**
Gro. **$10.00**

L8136—Cup 4x2, saucer, clear white china, conventional flower and leaf border, bright colorings, wide black band, blue flower and green leaf inlay, gold line handle. Matches L8348 plate. 1 doz. box..............Doz. **95c**

L8113 — Cup 4 x 2, saucer 5½, clear white china, small pink and green flower cluster and leaf wreath, black band with tan and blue inlay, gold line hdl., matches L8357 plate and L8141 3 pc. set. 1 doz. pkg..................Doz. **96c**

L8112—Cup 4x2, saucer 5½, clear white, transparent, painted pink carnation & toned green leaf wreath, gold line edges and hdl., matches L8140 3 pc. set. 1 doz. pkg.........Doz. **$1.25**

AFTER DINNER CUPS AND SAUCERS.

1 doz. pkg.

L1530— Cup 3x1⅝, saucer 4¼ in., Mino ware china, all over blue decoration. Doz. **42c**

L7060—2⅞x1¾, saucer 4¼, allover flowers and figures. enamel traced, Tokio red edges and handle. Doz. **72c**

L7578—Cup 3x2½, saucer 5, enamel traced Japanese figured and floral landscape, Tokio red edge and hdls. Doz. **89c**

FANCY BONBON OR OLIVE DISHES.

L5060 — 5½ in., ribbed, clear white china, 3 hand painted floral decorations, gold ornamented. cobalt edges. 1 doz. pkg. Doz. **89c**

L8320 — 7½, ribbed, gold illuminated Japanese figure and garden scene, gold ornamented Tokio red edge and feet. ¼ doz. pkg. Doz. **$2.00**

SAUCE OR FRUIT DISHES.

L8230    L8231

L8230—5¼ in., paneled, Japanese figure and garden decor., Tokio red edge. 1 doz. pkg. Doz. **72c**

L8231—5¼ in., ribbed, white china, conventional floral and leaf wreath, black border, blue floral inlay. 1 doz. pkg... ...Doz. **85c**

FOOTED NUT BOWLS.

L8250—4½, ribbed, lt. tan tint, pink flower and green leaf bouquets, blue & gold bands, lt. blue border, gold lined edge. 1 doz. pkg. Doz. **89c**

L7657   L7668

L7657 — 5¾ in., scallop panels, allover Jap figures and flower garden, Tokio red edge and feet. 1 doz. pkg..............Doz. **96c**
L7668—7 in. bulge panels, characteristic Japanese tea garden, floral border, Tokio red scallop edge and feet. ½ doz. pkg. Doz. **$1.95**

SALAD OR BERRY BOWL.

L7102—8½ in., floral garland and lantern framed garden and lake scene, Tokio red edge. 3 in pkg. .Each, **29c**

SALAD OR BERRY SET.

1 set in pkg.

L7793 — Bowl 8½ in., SIX individual nappies 5 in., embossed all over Japanese figure and landscape decoration, enamel studded cherry blossoms, Tokio red edge. 1 set pkg. Set, **65c**

SUGAR AND CREAM SET.

L7758 — Sugar 5½, creamer 4½, allover Japanese figures and landscape, Tokio red edges, knobs and hdls. 3 sets pkg.....Set, **25c**

SALT AND PEPPER SHAKERS.

Each with cork. 1 dz.box, 6 salts, 6 peppers.

L7032    L6181    L7743    L7165

L7032—3 in., 2 styles Japanese scene, floral border, Tokio red top and base.....Doz. **32c**
L6181—3½x2¼, allover Japanese decoration cobalt top & base, gold ornamented. Doz. **42c**
L7743—2 styles, 3½ in., ribbed, lt. green tints, current and grape decors., shaded green foliage. gold ornamented cobalt band, gold decorated top.................Doz. **45c**

L7165—3½ in., paneled, pastel tints, cherry trees, gold line neck and base.....................Doz. **69c**

L8185

L8185—3 in., hexagon, clear white china, gold outlined pink roses and leaves, beaded gold scrolls, gold decorated top and line base. Doz. **85c**

FOOTED NUT SET.

L7801—Dish 7½, six bowls 3 in. ribbed melon shape, Japanese figure and tea house decoration, floral border in bright colors, gold ornamented cobalt edges and feet. 1 set box, 3 sets pkg....................Set, **39c**

BLUE CHINA BOWL—1 doz. pkg.

L1740—4¼x2¼, fire proof all over blue outside decoration birds and flowers, band round inner top and bottom. Doz. **36c**

LOW CRACKER OR BISCUIT JAR.

L7720—7½ x 4¼, enamel traced rose cluster and forget me nots, gold outlined enamel studded inlays, gold ornamented cobalt blue knobs, edges and hdls. Ea. **39c**

HIGH CRACKER OR BISCUIT JAR.

L8390—6x5¼, allover Japanese figure and garden scene, Tokio red edges, gold line handle. 2 in pkg. Each, **39c**

TABLE PLATES.

L1625—7½ in. clear white china, blue and white peonies. 1 doz. pkg. Doz. **89c**

L8348—7¼ in., clear white china, conventional flower and leaf border, bright colorings, wide black band, blue flower and green leaf inlay, gold line handle. Matches L8136 cup and saucer. 1 doz. box. Doz. **92c**

L8357—7¼, clear white, pink and green small flower and leaf border, wide black edge, blue & tan inlay, matches L8113 cup & saucer. 1 doz. pkg. Doz. **96c**

L8356—7¼, clear white china, pink carnation and shaded green leaf wreath, gold line edge, matches L8112 cup and saucer and L8140 3 pc. set. 1 doz. pkg......Doz. **98c**

TEA STRAINER.

L7848—5½ in. deep, 3 feet, allover blue & white Sometsuke decoration. 1 doz. pkg. Doz. **89c**

JAPANESE CHINA CHOCOLATE SETS.

Chocolate pot and 6 cups and saucers.

L9195—Pot 10 in., cups 2½x3, saucers 5, paneled, allover Japanese figure and floral landscape, Tokio red edges, knob and hdls. 1 set in box. Set, **85c** ½ doz. or more, **$9.00** doz. sets.

L9202—Pot 10 in., cups 2¼x3, saucers 5 in., paneled, lt. tan tints, gold ornamented pink & green poppies and leaves, gold edges, dec. hdls. and cover. 1 set in box.....Set, **$1.35**

L9201—Pot 10 in., cups 2¼x3, saucers 5 in., paneled, clear white, black outlined pink conventional blossoms and green leaves, lt. blue band, gold dec. cobalt edges, knob and hdls. 1 set in box. Set, **$1.10** ½ doz. or more, **$11.40** doz. sets.

L9199—Pot 9½ in., cups 2½x3 saucers 5, rib panels, ivory tint, embossed all gold flower and leaf medallions, beaded gold framing, gold bands, dec. hdls. and knob. 1 set in box. Set, **$1.95**

12 STYLES HAND PAINTED PORCELAIN VASE ASST.

L9297—Aver. 9 in., 12 styles, pastel tints, all gold ornaments, 4 landscape and 8 floral designs, elaborate gold borders, dec. hlds. and necks. 1 doz. in case, asstd..............Doz. **$4.50**

VASE ASSORTMENT.

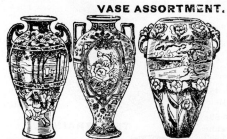

L9073—Ht. 16 in., girth 24 in., 6 styles, fancy shapes, tinted grounds, **hand painted**, landscape and floral medallions, embossed gold frames, gold ornamented, floral and conventional borders, gold covered handles. 1 pr. each style, 1 doz. in case...........................Doz. **$13.00**

Butler Bros., Catalog #1208, 1914

BREAD AND BUTTER PLATES.

L6820—6 in., allover blue Sometsuke. 1 doz. pkg. Doz. **45c**

L7615—6 in., characteristic Japanese landscape design, floral border, fluted flange, Tokio red edge. 1 doz. in pkg. Doz. **69c**

L7620—6 in., Japanese landscape and flower garden, cherry trees and blossoms, fluted flange, gold ornamented cobalt blue edge. 1 doz. in pkg...............Doz. **85c**

COMBINATION STRAINER.

L9425—6 in., 2 styles, gold framed violet and rose medallions, ivory tinted band, gold dec. inlays, center ornaments and foot, beaded gold edges. Consists of tea strainer and drip holder to match. ½ doz. box, asstd... Doz. **$2.25**

TABLE PLATES.

L5008—7¼ in., allover Japanese figure and landscape decor., Tokio red edge. 1 doz. in pkg. Doz. **79c**

L9131—7¼ in., all blue Sometsuke conventional floral border. Matches L9129 cup and saucer. 1 doz. in pkg. Doz. **95c**

CAKE PLATES.

L7627—8½ in., clear white, enamel traced Japanese scene in bright colors, profuse gold work, gold scroll and band on cobalt edge. ½ doz. in pkg....Doz. **$2.10**

L9316—9½ in., enamel traced large poppy and leaf wreath, dec. cobalt edges and open hdls. 3 in box.........EACH, **39c**

TOOTHPICK HOLDERS.

L9121 **L9122**

L9121—2¼ in., clear white ribbed, small rose and leaf wreath, black border, Tokio red edge. 1 doz. in pkg. Doz. **32c**

L9122—1¾ in., clear white, hand painted rose and leaf cluster, gold ornamentation, cobalt edge. 1 doz. in box. Doz. **39c**

EGG CUPS.

L9125 **L5037**

L9125—1¾x2¼, bright color flower and leaf wreath, Tokio red borders, colored inlays. 1 doz. in box.. ....Doz. **25c**

L5037—2¾x3½, allover Japanese scene, Tokio red and gold edges. 1 doz. in pkg. Doz. **69c**

19 STYLES JAP CHINA ASSORTMENT.

Made up in Japan from merchandise especially selected for the purpose—all fresh, attractive merchandise, no odds and ends in these lots. You get a big variety of classy goods with very moderate investment and you avoid the trouble of selecting.

L1000—Variety Asst. 19 styles, comprises chocolate, berry and tea sets, cups and saucers, plates, mustard pot, nut bowls, sugar shakers, hair receivers, puff boxes, salts and peppers and hat pin holders. Allover Japanese landscape decorations, Tokio red edges, hand painted floral designs, gold ornamented, cups and saucers count as 1 pc. Retails from 10 to 50c each. 12 doz. case...........................Complete, **$10.68** Doz. **89c**

JAPANESE CHINA SUGAR AND CREAM SETS.

L9135—Sugar 4¾, creamer 3, buff sharkskin bodies, raised green and white enamel floral decor. ½ doz. sets in pkg. DOZ. SETS, **$1.85**

L7758 — Sugar 5½, creamer 4½, allover Japanese figures and landscape, Tokio red edges, knobs and hdls. 3 sets in pkg. Set, **25c**

L9229—Sugar 6¼, creamer 5¼, clear white, pink & blue flower and leaf border design, enamel studded blue band, gold line edges, dec. handles and knob. 1 set in box...Set, **33c**

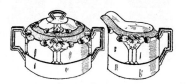

L9219—Sugar 5½, creamer 4½, mission shape, clear white, black outlined conventional blue and red maple leaves on buff border between gold bands, gold dec. handles and knob. 1 set in box.................... Set, **39c**

4 PC. TABLE SET.

L9435—Sugar, creamer, butter, spoon holder clear white, large pink wild roses, green leaves, maroon bands, gold lined edges, hdl., dec. knobs. 1 set in box......Set, **75c**

SAUCE OR FRUIT DISHES.

L9497—5½ in., ribbed, enamel traced Japanese figure and landscape design, brown edge. 1 dz. in pkg...........Doz. **75c**

TOOTH BRUSH HOLDER.

L9123—4¼x2¼, clear white, scenic decor., green edges. 1 doz. in pkg.............Doz. **75c**

JAPANESE CHINA 3 PIECE TABLE SETS.

Teapot, sugar and creamer.

L1598—Tea pot 4¼, sugar 3¾, creamer 3, buff sharkskin bodies, raised green & white enameled floral decoration... .....Set, **25c**

L9517 — Teapot 7 in., sugar 5½, creamer 4½, allover japanese figure and floral landscape Tokio red edges... ....Set, **39c**
L8775—Tea set with 6 cups and saucers, as L9517............................Complete, **85c**

L9133 — Teapot 7½, sugar 5½, creamer 4½, clear white, conventional grape and leaf border, wide black band, gold line edges and hdls., gold dec. spout and knobs.....Set, **50c**
L8776 — Tea with 6 cups and saucers, as L9133...... .... Complete, **$1.00**

L9151 — Teapot 7½, sugar 5½, creamer 4½, clear white, enamel traced pink and yellow roses and green leaves, green Grecian band, gold edges, dec. hdls., knobs and spout. Set, **69c**
L8778—Tea set with 6 cups and saucers, as L9151.........................Complete, **$1.35**

SUGAR SHAKER.

L9420—4 x 4¾, clear **white**, paneled, pink and blue conventional blossoms and green leaves, tan and black border, gold dec. top and line handle. 1 doz. in box..........Doz. **92c**

SYRUP PITCHER.

L9470—Pitcher 5¼, saucer 5½, conventional pink flower and green leaf border, tan b a n d, small pink flowers on black band, gold edges, dec. handle and knob. ½ doz. in box.
Doz. **$2.25**

FANCY BONBON OR OLIVE DISHES.

L5060—5½ in., ribbed, clear white china 3 hand painted floral decorations, gold ornamented cobalt edges. 1 doz. in pkg ... .Doz. Out

L8320—7½ ribbed, gold illuminated Japanese figure and garden scene, gold ornamented Tokio red edge and feet. ½ doz. in pkg.........Doz. **$2.00**

L9373—7¾ in., footed, ribbed, lt. blue tint, berry, leaf and bird decor., beaded green edge. 3 in box...EACH, **25c**

L9382 — 4 styles, average 7 in., bisque finish, wild rose decoration, gold ornamented pink and blue floral design, pastel tint landscape, embossed gold roses. All with gold edges, handles or feet. 4 in pkg., asstd..EACH, **39c**

L9378—8 in., bisque finish, **hand painted** pastel landscape, gold and tan border, enamel ornaments gold covered open handles. 1 in box.
EACH, **72c**

Butler Bros., Catalog #1208, 1914

7 PC. BERRY OR ICE CREAM SET.

Consists of large bowl and SIX individual dishes.

L2229—Bowl 8½, saucers 5, Japanese landscape and tea house decoration, floral framing, variegated colors, red edge, gold ornaments. 1 set in box.............................. Set

SPOON TRAY OR PICKLE DISH.

L2436—9⅜ in., lt. tan border, gold outlined, red and lavender floral and leaf sprays with connecting stems, gold beaded edge, gold center medallion. ¼ doz. in box. .Doz. **$3.60**

7 PC. CELERY SET.

Large tray, SIX individual salt dips.

L2254—Gold and white. Tray 10⅞, ind. 3¾, open handles, heavily embossed and beaded floral design, beaded edge. 1 set in box..Set. **$1.25**

SUGAR SHAKERS.

L2480—4x4¾, paneled trailing blossom and leaf spray, conventional band border, gold lined edges and handle, gold starred top. 1 doz. in box........ ....Doz. **96c**

SCREW TOP

L9421—5 in., ivory tinted, paneled, gold outlined pink lotus blossoms and green leaves beaded gold band. gold dec. top and line base. 3 in box.
EACH. **36c**

FOOTED BONBON OR NUT BOWL.

L9373—7⅝ in., footed, ribbed, lt. blue tint, berry, leaf and bird decor., beaded green edge. ¼ doz. in box. Doz. **$2.25**

Butler Bros., Catalog #1288, 1915

"VARIETY" ASSORTMENT,

L3000 — "Variety" Asst. 19 styles, comprises chocolate, berry and tea sets, cups and saucers, plates, mustard pots, nut bowls and dishes, bonbon boxes and hair receivers, sugar shakers, salts and peppers and hatpin holders. White china, gold or enamel traced hand painted floral and Japanese landscape decors. Cup and saucer count as 1 pc. Retail range 10c to $1.00. (Total for asst. **$9.00**) 12 doz. in case, 125 lbs. Doz. **75c**

6 of 9 styles

L2020—Ht. 10 in., asstd. shapes, tinted or mottled bodies, floral and landscape decors., gold framings, borders, ornamentation & hdls., **9 styles**, 2 prs. each. 3 dz. case, 150 lbs. Dz. **$3.75**

L2023—Ht. 15 in., girth 24 in., fancy shapes, tinted grounds, **hand painted** floral backs or landscape panels, embossed gold frames, floral and gold borders, gold handles. **6 styles** 1 pr. each. 1 doz. in case, 160 lbs....... ....Doz. **$7.50**

BERRY BOWL.

2 of 3 styles

L2425 — 3 styles, average 8⅝ in., profusely gold ornamented floral designs on tinted ground, gold beaded or ornamented oriental band borders. Asstd. ¼ doz. in box. Doz. **$3.75**

FOOTED NUT BOWLS.

2 of 3 styles

L2343—3 styles, 4½ in., scalloped edge, enamel traced or gold ornamented floral designs, beaded enamelor gold band edges, gold ornamented feet. Asstd. 1 doz. in pkg. Doz. **78c**

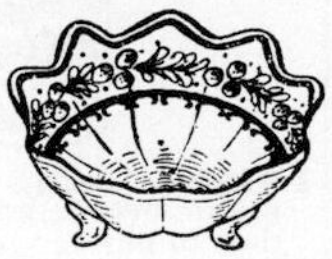

L2344—5½ in., fluted, tinted leaf and berry cluster wreath between enamel studded bands, gold ornamented center, edge and feet. 1 doz. in pkg. Doz. **89c**

FOOTED NUT SETS.

Set consists of 1 large dish and SIX individual bowls.

L8268—Dish 5¾, bowls 2¾, allover Japanese landscape decor. Tokio red edges and feet. ⅓ doz. sets in pkg. Doz. sets. **$2.20**

L2205—Dish 6, bowls 3¼, red, pink & blue flower and leaf scroll, green Grecian band, gold edge. ⅓ doz. sets in box................Doz. sets. **$3.60**

FANCY DECORATED JAP CHINA TABLE AND TEA SETS.

Very special values at the price.

Japanese Landscape—Black enamel traced landscape, green & white enamel studded trees, gold edges and line hdls. 1 set in box.

L4023—3 Pc. Set. Tea pot ht. 5½, sugar ht. 4¾, creamer ht. 3¾..............Set, 67c

L5011—9 Pc. Set. 3 Pc. Set with 6 cups and saucers.......... .. ..Set, $1.25

JAP CHINA SUGAR AND CREAM SETS.

L2312—Sugar ht. 3¼, creamer ht. 3⅜, buff sharkskin bodies, raised green and white enamel floral decor. ½ doz. sets in pkg.
Doz. sets, $2.25

L4102—Sugar ht. 4⅛, creamer ht. 3, Japanese figures and landscapes, Tokio red edges, knob and hdl. ½ doz. sets in pkg. **Temp. Out**
Doz. sets

L2301—Sugar ht. 4¼, creamer ht. 2¾, blue and crimson dahlias on leaf and tendril scroll border, gold band edges, knob and hdls. ½ doz. sets. in box...........Doz. sets, $3.75

HAND PAINTED JAPANESE CUP, SAUCER AND PLATE.

Unusually attractive decorations. Big sellers.

Wild Rose—White enamel outlined wild rose wreath, trailing vine and shaded foliage, heavy gold band and tracing, gold line hdl. 1 doz. in box.

L4049—Cup & saucer. Cup 3¾ x 2, saucer 5½ in. Doz. **$1.08**

L4050—Plate. 7¼ in. Doz. **Temp-Out**

JAP CHINA FOOTED NUT BOWL.

L4258 — 3 shapes. Aver. 5 in., pink & blue floral wreaths or sprays, enamel or gold decorations, gold edges and ornamented feet. 1 doz. in box. **Temp-Out**

JAP CHINA TOOTH PICK HOLDER.

L4411—3 styles. 2½ in., ribbed, gold ornamented blue border, rose and blossom decorations, gold line edges. Asstd, 2 doz. in box. **Temp-Out**

JAP CHINA "VARIETY" ASSORTMENT.

L4000—"Variety" Asst. 19 styles. Comprises chocolate, berry and tea sets, cups & saucers (*count as 1 pc. each*) plates, mustard pots, nut bowls and dishes, puff box & hair receivers, sugar shakers, salts & peppers, hat pin holders. White china, gold or enamel traced hand painted floral and Japanese landscape decors. Retail range 10c to $1.00. 12 doz. in shipping case. 125 lbs..Doz. **89c**
(Total for asst. $10.20.)

Allover Jap Design—Figure and floral landscape, Tokio red edges. 1 set in box.
L9517—3 Pc. Set. Tea pot ht. 4¾, sugar ht. 3¾ in., creamer ht. 3 .... Temp Out
L9692—9 Pc. Set. 3 Pc. Set, with 6 cups and saucers..........................Temp-Out

HAND PAINTED PORCELAIN VASE ASSORTMENT.

L4461—6 styles. Jap porcelain, aver. 9½ in., pastel tints, hand painted, 2 landscape, 4 floral subjects, gold outlined conventional or floral borders, gold edges and hdls. 1 doz. in case, 49 lbs.. .... Temp Out

Butler Bros., Catalog #1410, 1916

IMPORTED CHINA ASSORTMENT

L6574—24 styles, (each set counts as 1 pc.), pink & crimson blossom and foliage clusters with connecting twigs forming wreath, gold tracings and dec. amber border, center spray, gold hdls. and edges. Asst. comprises salad bowls, cake plates, utility bowls, sugar & creamer, chocolate, berry and cake sets, bonbon or jewel box with tray, tankard, celery, nut and dresser sets, vases, candlesticks. Asstd. 24 pcs. in case, 115 lbs. (Total for asst. $18.00) **Each, 75c**

JAP CHINA VASE ASSORTMENTS

L5977—6 styles, 6 to 7½ in., 2 landscapes, 4 floral decors., tinted grounds, gold traced or enamel beaded borders and handles. Asstd. 1 doz. in case, 35 lbs. Temp. Out

L5978 — 6 styles, aver. 7 to 8¾ in., pastel tints, 4 scenic, 2 gold traced floral designs, conventional borders, enamel or gold traced and beaded. Asstd. 1 doz. in case, 35 lbs. **Doz. $8.25**

MISCELLANEOUS ASSORTMENT

L2700 — 6 styles, nut bowls, bonbons and salt dips, aver. size 3x1½, asstd. shapes, floral designs, gold border, all trademarked, band painted. Asstd. 2 doz. in pkg........Doz. **48c** (Total for asst. 96c)

7 PC. CAKE SET

L6241—Dish 9½, SIX plates 6½, lt. blue & gold band with pink rose inlays, outer gold band, beaded edge. 1 set in pkg...SET (7 pcs.), **$1.65**

DRESSER SET

3 Pc—Tray 7¾x3¼, hair receiver and puff jar, 3¾x2½, dome covers, embossed, enamel traced pink floral sprays, gold tendrils and edges.
L6430—2 sets in pkg...SET, ★**45** (Total 90 c)

5 PC. DRESSER SET

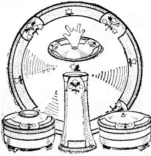

L6435—5 pc., tray 9⅝, hatpin holder 5⅝, footed hair receiver and puff jar 3¾x2⅛, ring tree 4 in., pink and ivory panel border, floral medallions, gold tracings and feet. 1 set in pkg.
SET (5 pcs.), **$1.35**

HAIR RECEIVER AND PUFF BOX

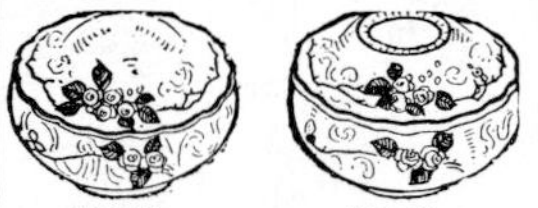

L6417   **L6418**

3¾x2½ in. dome covers, pink blossom sprays with connecting green vine. 1 doz. in pkg.

L6417—Puff box......} Doz.
L6418—Hair receiver.} **$1.35**

PIN OR ASH TRAY ASST.

L5950—6 styles, aver. 4x3¼, floral and landscape decors., gold and enamel tracings. Asstd. 1 doz. in pkg.
Doz. 85c

HATPIN HOLDER

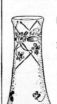

L7530—5½ in., forget-me-not decoration with spray and fancy gold trimming, gold lined edges. 1 doz. in pkg.
Doz. 96c

---

4 PC. SMOKERS' SET

L6535—4 pcs., tray 7⅛, cigar holder 2⅞, match holder 1⅝, ash tray 2½, white enamel traced brown band, allover Japanese scenic design. 1 set in box.
SET (4 pcs.), ★**56**

TOBACCO JAR ASST.

L1081—2 styles, white china, allover tinted tan to brown, playing card and horses head decors., beaded edges. Asstd. 2 in pkg...... Each, **95c** (Total for asst. $1.90)

3 PC. MAYONNAISE SETS

L6376—Bowl 4¾ in., ladle 5, tray 5½, white enamel dec. tan border with pendants, rosebud sprays, gold ornaments, edge dec. hdl. and feet. ½ doz. sets in pkg.
Doz. sets, $4.10

CHEESE AND CRACKER SETS

L716-3—Covered cheese and tray attached covered cheese container 1⅝x4¼, white china, forget-me-not sprays, gold dec. knobs and edges. 1 in pkg........Each, ★**69**

Butler Bros., Catalog #1696, 1919

40

BERRY SETS

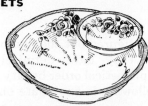

E4934 — Bowl 8⅞ in., 6 berries 5⅜, good quality light wt. china, pink tinted chrysanthemum centers, dk. green & ivory luster, scroll embossed edge, shaded foliage. 1 set in pkg.............Set, **$2.25**

E6162 — Bowl 10 in., 6 fruits 4¾ in., pink and red rose spray, light green and gold line edge. 1 set in pkg. Set, **$2.75**

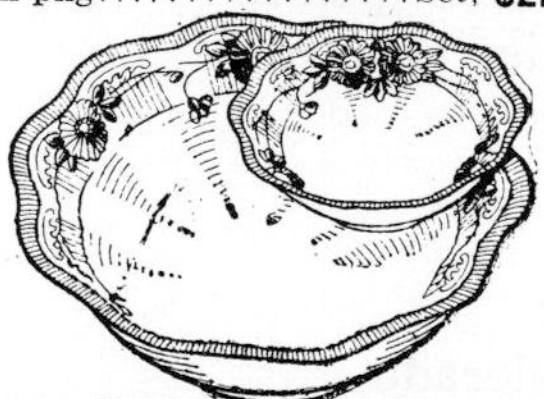

E6160 — Bowl 8½ in., 6 fruits 5 in., fluted hand painted floral inside border, cream colored band, gold line tracing and narrow line edge. 1 set in pkg............ Set, **$2.25**

E6163 — Bowl 9¾ in., 6 fruits 5⅞ in., good quality, pure white, highly glazed, blue and pink floral and foliage sprays, gold scroll outlined ivory band, gold edges. 1 set in pkg. Set, **$2.85**

7 PC. IMPORTED CHINA CELERY SET

E6161 — Bowl 10 in., 6 fruits 4¾ in., large floral spray, light tan band and gold line edge. 1 set in pkg. Set, **$2.75**

E7315 — Dish 7¼ in., 6 indvs. 2⅜ in., pink floral spray with connecting gold band, gold edge, white china. ¼ doz. sets in pkg. Doz. sets, **$4.50**

IMPORTED CHINA TOY TEA SETS

E7595 E5692 E7596 E5668

E7595—13 pcs., pink flowers and landscape scenes, gold ornamentations, 5½ x 4¼ partitioned box. 1 doz. sets in pkg. .Doz. sets, **$1.75**

E7596—14 pcs., pink oriental flowers, blue and bronze illuminations, 6¾x5¼ partitioned box. 1 doz. sets in pkg.........Doz. sets, **$2.25**

E5692—9 pcs., asstd. pink conventional decors. with blue ribbon bowknots, gold ornamentations, 6½x4¼ partitioned box. Asstd. 1 doz. sets in pkg. Doz. sets, **$2.10**

E5668—23 pcs., 2 decors., one allover green landscape scene, other pink and blue oriental flowers, blue enameled border, 10½x6¾ partitioned box. Asstd. ¼ doz. sets in pkg.............Doz. sets, **$6.75**

7 PC. IMPORTED CHINA CHOCOLATE SET

E5479—Pot 9½ in., 6 cups, 2⅜x3 in., saucers 5 in., fancy Japanese tea garden decoration, variegated colors, red edges, gold loops, red handles. 1 set in pkg
SET (7 pcs.), **$2.75**

E5465—Sugar 3¾ in., creamer 3 in., gold outlined, small tea rose cluster and gold leaves on ivory wide band, studded gold borders between decors., gold lined handles. ½ doz. sets in pkg.........Doz. sets, **$10.50**

IMPORTED CHINA HAIR RECEIVER

E5651—3¾ x 2¼ in., paneled, embossed, blue floral sprays on tinted ground. 1 doz. in pkg...Doz. **$1.75**

CAKE SETS

E6170—Dish 9½ in., 6 plates, 6¼ in., floral spray, light tan and gold line edge. 1 set in pkg......Set, **$2.75**

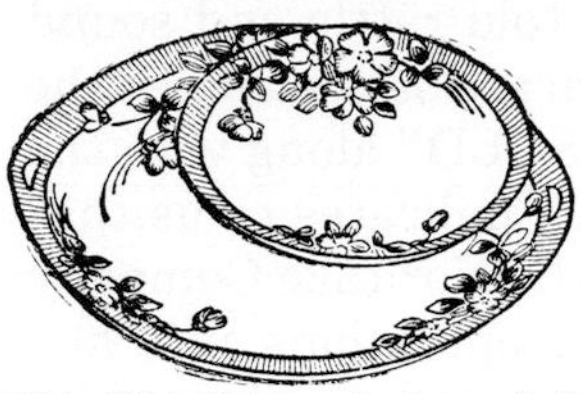

E6171—Dish 9½ in., 6 plates, 6 in. pink and red rose spray, light green band edge, gold lined. 1 set in pkg. Set, **$2.75**

IMPORTED CHINA SPOON TRAY ASSORTMENT

E5640—3 styles, aver. 7½ in., fancy shape, full floral borders, gold verge lines, some with cutout handles. Asstd. ½ doz. in pkg. Doz. **$2.75**

E5643—3 styles, 8¼x3¾, light wt. china body, rose, forget-me-not and wild blossom sprays, blue borders, gold edges, cut-out handles. Asstd. ½ doz. in pkg.......Doz. **$6.50**

JOINTED BISQUE DOLLS

F9788-9657 F8176

Special—Flesh tinted, stout bodies, painted curly hair, features, shoes and stockings.
F9788—2¾ in. 1 doz. in box............Temp. Out
F9651 — 3¾ in. 1 doz. in box....Doz. **65c**
F9653—6⅝ in. ½ doz. in box..........Doz. **$1.75**
F9657—7¼ in. ½ doz. in box..........Doz. **$2.25**
F8176 — 4½ in. flesh tinted body, painted hair features, shoes and stockings. 1 doz. in box.
6 doz. lots. Doz. **78c**
(Total $4.68)

"BABY BUD" BISQUE DOLLS

A chubby little figure with roguish expression and arms that can be moved with many cute poses.

Fine flesh tinted bisque, painted features, roguish eyes, exposed tongue, short shirt, movable position arms which give different expressions at each pose, each in box.
F9806—4 in. 1 doz. in pkg. Doz. **$1.35**
F9808—6¾ in. ½ doz. in pkg. Doz. **$3.75**

PENNY SOLID CHINA DOLL

White china body painted features, blonde and brunette hair. 1 gro. in box.
F9780—1¾ in. Gro. **65c**
F9781—2½ in. Gro. **89c**

GLAZED SOLID CHINA DOLL

F8175 — 2 in., glazed white body, painted features, hair, shoes and stockings. 6 doz. in box..........Doz. **22c**
(Total $1.32)

BABY DOLL IN BATH TUB

F9786—1¾ in., sitting detachable baby, painted hair and features, white china 2⅜ in. tub, heavy gilt rim. 1 doz. in box..........Doz. **75c**

Butler Bros., Catalog #1280, 1920

NIPPON NOTES AND TRIVIA

Collectors will sometimes find a two-piece item marked with a gold symbol or number inside. This was done at the factory to enable the workers to match up a top and bottom to insure a proper fit. Many times collectors think this "mark" is merely a dab of paint that went astray but if one looks closely enough, we often discover that the marks match on the two pieces.

For collectors who want to know the difference be—tween a hanging wall plaque and a plate, turn the item over. A plaque will be pierced on the reverse side for hanging. Nothing prevents plates from decorating walls, but it is necessary to provide a proper holder for these pieces.

One of my researchers discovered a lovely Nippon scenic bottle vase. It has a cork at the top and there are contents inside which I am told rattle and sound a little bit like rice. On the bottom are backstamped the words "SAMPLE NOT TO BE SOLD" along with the familiar M in wreath mark which indicates to us that this item was manufactured by the Noritake Company which took over the Morimura operations in 1904. Evidently some of our Nippon items were once used by the salesmen only for display. Wouldn't it be interesting to uncork the bottle after all these years and find out what is inside?

The Nippon Nipper is still a popular item since we first mentioned its existence in Series II. We still have not figured out the numbering system of these pieces as they have definitely not been numbered in alphabetical order by city or by the size of the city. The following is an update on the Nippon Nipper:

#13 Lowell, Massachusetts
#20 New London, Connecticut
#24 White Mountain, New Hampshire
#27 Scranton, Pennsylvania
#35 Watertown, New York
#36 Cincinnati, Ohio
#42 Syracuse, New York
#221 Burlington, Vermont
#247 Colorado Springs, Colorado
#920 Westerly, Rhode Island

Since we know that the numbers run all the way up to 920 and possibly beyond, it leads us to speculate that there were quite a few Nippers produced years ago. They are marked as souvenirs but we still wonder why Nipper was depicted on them. Perhaps, someday the mystery will be solved.

Dolls beguile collectors and add a nice touch to any collection. We have found a Little Red Riding Hood, a baseball player, Manikin dolls, bathtub dolls, soldiers and Happifats. There seems to be a doll for every type of doll collector and collectors have learned to display them in the most interesting ways.

Nipper pin dish, Souvenir of Colorado Springs, Colorado

Salesman's sample vase

Bottom of salesman's sample vase showing paper label affixed over green M in wreath mark.

A variety of small bisque dolls.

"PRE" NIPPON??

A good friend of mine, Jess Berry, wrote an article on so-called "pre" Nippon for a newspaper I edited. He was kind enough to give me permission to include it in this publication. His views parallel mine and I thought his article was very meaningful to collectors.

What does the term "Pre-Nippon" mean to you? This description is frequently applied to unmarked items which appear to be Japanese regardless of quality, style or workmanship. In some instances this connotation is correct -- however, more often than not the items so described are later than the Nippon period.

There are, of course, many wonderful pieces of Nippon which are for one reason or another unmarked. Some may have been one of a pair or part of a set, with only a piece or two bearing the Nippon mark. Other items possibly entered the U.S. via a circuitous route through a country not requiring the backstamp. Such pieces are Nippon without the "pre".

Unfortunately, many of the pieces advertised as "pre-Nippon" are inferior copies of earlier items by the makers themselves. Technically, any item produced in Japan could be classified as Nippon, but for the purposes of Nippon collecting, the time span is clearly defined, and the pieces produced later do not fall into this category. There are assuredly some fine items in circulation from the later period but most of those regularly found with the "pre-Nippon" tagging are of a quality below the older standard.

An experienced collector can usually spot the difference between originals and the later wares, and can form his own opinion on the "pre" classification of un-marked items. The beginning Nippon collector unfortunately may not be as quick to spot diffences and could be paying Nippon prices for less-than-quality items.

As for those who are so quick to advertise something as "pre-Nippon", I think in many cases it is lack of knowledge rather than intent to mislead. Anyone with something for sale tries to identify the merchandise and therein lies the danger. If it resembles Nippon, it must be Nippon; but, without a mark, the tendency is to assume it was from an earlier period.

When purchasing an unmarked item, use your experience, common sense and instinct. Study carefully and compare jeweling, moriage and the use of gold. Inspect the artwork closely and don't forget to note the weight and feel of the piece.

There is nothing wrong with a good unmarked item - my collection has several, some really excellent. However, I have some items from the early years of collecting that are not from the Nippon era, and definitely not "pre-Nippon" as they were advertised. I think it all comes down to one thing - don't be too much influenced by other opinions -- if you really fall in love with a piece, it doesn't much matter about the mark, but be alert and consider carefully. Remember, buy what you like and not what someone tells you should be in your collection.

COLLECTING THE UNUSUAL

Many collectors do not specialize in any one category of Nippon but prefer to collect one or two of everything and the more unusual the better. They seek out knife rests, sugar sifters, desk items, potpourri jars, napkin rings, cinnamon stick holders, the list goes on and on. And what an intriguing hobby this can be. Not only are they collecting Nippon, but they are also studying the dining habits and customs of long ago. Can you just imagine their joy when finding something really unique, a porcelain rolling pin perhaps!

Some of these types of items are, of course, still used in households today; but unless you dine with kings and queens, it's doubtful that you bring out the individual salt dips each night - or bone dishes or sugar sifters. And how many of you ladies can't survive without your hair receiver or hatpin holder? Very few, I'm sure. But it is fun and interesting to find out the past use of these pieces.

Today we just naturally think of a cup and saucer as one article - "useless each without the other." Yet it has only been since the latter part of the eighteenth century that saucers were introduced. At first, persons using them were greatly ridiculed, and it was said that they were not able to drink without two cups. How things have changed since then.

In Rudolph Brasch's book *How Did It Begin?*, he says that originally there was no difference between the tea and coffee pots. Everyone wanted to acquire a Chinese atmosphere and it was fashionable to copy the wide and bulky Chinese porcelain teapots for both coffee and tea. Later, however, changes were made in the pots. "A low, wide pot provides for the maximum expansion of the tea leaves which, being light, tend to rise in hot water. On the other hand, soon after boiling water has been poured on coffee, the grounds sink to the bottom and pure clean coffee is left in the rest of the pot. Its narrow, high shape thus serve it best."

From the Ceramic Art Co. catalog, circa 1910, the following information was discovered on loving cups, "In the good old days 'lang syne,' kings were regarded as the cleverest and the best of men. They created the most useful inventions and established many of the most beautiful customs. Therefore it is not surprising that tradition should positively assert that the idea of the loving cups first originated in a royal brain.

"The time and nationality of the kingly inventor is not recorded with certainty — he may have been Henry V of England, or Henry IV of Navarre. It is tolerably certain, however, that it was one or the other of those famous kings who developed the idea as the result of a curious experience.

"As the story goes, he was out hunting one day, when he became separated from his companions, and rode alone in the forest until he was very thirsty. Suddenly he came upon a wayside inn and demanded a cup of wine, and in obedience to his imperial call, an awkward little serving-maid came forward holding the cup by the handle in such a manner that when it was passed to the king, a portion of the wine was spilled on his majesty's gloves.

"King Henry rode away refreshed, but his soiled gloves set him thinking, with the result that he arrived at the conclusion that a cup with two handles would prevent a recurrence of the mishap, and as soon as possible he ordered such a cup made at once at the royal potteries and had it sent to the inn.

"When next he stopped at the little hostelry and called for wine, he was served by the same little maid, who, in passing the wine to his majesty grasped both handles of the cup in fear and trembling, lest she break it. The astonished king lost another pair of gloves, but found a way out of his perplexity by having a third handle added to the next cup which he sent to the inn. 'Surely,' he said, 'out of three handles, I should be able to lay hold of one.' Such is the traditional story of the origin of the loving cup as we know it; but certain it is that long before King Henry's day, cups and mugs with more than one handle had been used as the drinking vessels in social bouts of good fellowship."

Today we find Nippon-era sandwich trays, egg servers, tea caddies, sugar trays and baskets, stamp boxes, calendar stands and even stationery holders.

Years ago a calendar stand could be bought separately or purchased with a complete desk set. The one shown in the photograph originally came with little cards about the weight of poster board. There were three different sizes and they were placed according to size in the holder with the month, date and day of the week showing. A simple flip of the cards kept the calendar up to date.

The photo of the rolling pin is not only a Nippon marked item but also a genuine piece of Canadiana. The overall length is 19¼" and the wooden handles appear to be lathe-turned maple which have been varnished. The porcelain body is 2¾" in diameter and 9¾" long, highly glazed over the advertising copy and on one end. The other end is not glazed and is marked with the green rising sun Nippon mark.

The rolling pin advertises the Ogilvie Flour Co. in Canada and is one of a thousand rolling pins purchased as a premium just prior to World War I. According to a 1965 issue of *The Ogilvie Miller*, the first set received by the company was made in Germany but before they could be used, World War I broke out, making them quite undesirable to the public. The company then decided to order 1,000 more, but this time from Japan, with instructions that an identical 1,000 be made.

The Japanese are great imitators and in compliance with the company's instructions, the 1,000 rolling pins were made so exact that even the original "Made in Germany" backstamp was placed on. The situation was finally explained and cleared up and another 1,000 manufactured and marked with Nippon as the country of origin. But would you believe the wooden handles were made of wood that was too soft so a Winnipeg wood turner was commissioned to produce new handles. The pins finally sold as a 50¢ premium. It took, 3,000 porcelain pins and 4,000 sets of handles before these items ever made it on the market and I would say that makes these pieces very special indeed.

Calendar stand showing day, date and month cards in place and with cards in place and with cards removed so relative size can be judged.

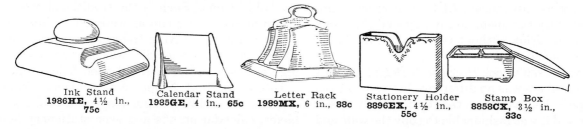

| Ink Stand
1986HE, 4½ in.,
75c | Calendar Stand
1985GE, 4 in., 65c | Letter Rack
1989MX, 6 in., 88c | Stationery Holder
8896EX, 4½ in.,
55c | Stamp Box
8858CX, 3½ in.,
33c |

An old ad for desk items.

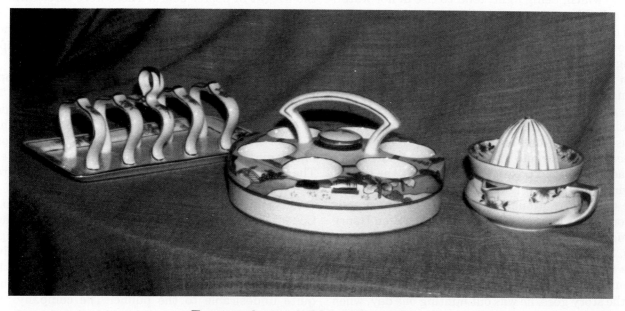

Toast rack, egg holder and reamer.

Egg server.

Sandwich tray.

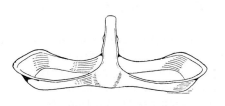

Ogilvie Flour rolling pin.

1026HT, dozen, 70c

1121ACX, doz., $1.33

Sandwich Basket
1341BDM, 11 inches, $2.48

Sugar Basket
1333SM, 5 inches, 98c

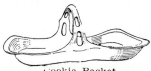

Cookie Basket
1137ACX, 7¾ in., $1.33

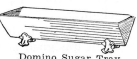

Domino Sugar Tray
1325HE, 6½ in., 75c

Cracker and Cheese Dish
1676ASM, 9½ inches, $1.98

Tea Caddy
1222GE, 4½ inches..............65c

Diameter of Tub, 5¾ inches
1653HC, 73c

Nut Dishes
1124ADM, 3 in., doz., $1.48

Breakfast Set

Tray is made of three-ply light basswood 18x12 inches, coated with foundation white. May be tinted with air-drying enamel colors to harmonize with decoration on china.

Trays improved by placing a light of glass over surface. Local dealers can supply at a small cost.

2635EXT, Set of 9 pieces, including tray..$5.50

Old ads showing a miscellany of unusual Nippon items.

PAGES OUT OF NIPPON'S PAST
by Helen and Bob Karlin
(used with permission of authors)

Even after 25 years of collecting and studying Nippon, we still can't ignore the challenge of trying to bridge any gap we encounter in our knowledge of this fascinating field.

Typical case in point: how did Nippon salesmen in America inform their prospects and customers* (wholesalers, department store buyers and mail-order houses) which items could be ordered and in what shapes, sizes, styles, scenes and patterns?

And how did Nippon-producing potteries keep their state-side representatives up to date on new selections, decor variations, changed color combinations, price changes, delivery dates and myriad other business details? (In *Japanese Ceramics Of the Last 100 Years*, Irene Stitt indicates that there were at least 300 commercial kilns operating in Honshu, Kyushu, Skikoku and other provinces during the Edo and Meiji periods.)

The search for answers to these and related questions began routinely enough as just another one of our self-motivated "homework assignments." It quickly escalated into a demanding but dramatically rewarding research experience.

A lot of time and travel, much detective work (including many dead-end leads and "cold trails") and more than a little luck eventually resulted in the surprising and exciting discovery of pages from a Nippon salesman's sample book.

Some of our "pages out of the past" have been used to illustrate this chapter. In a very real sense, they *are* the chapter.

There is little doubt that these exquisitely hand colored but unsigned paintings were made in Japan and annotated in America. Examination of the paper and paints indicate that they were of the type used during the Nippon period. [No doubt the reader is aware that Nippon was manufactured from 1891 to 1921, straddling the Meiji (1868-1912) and Taisho (1912-1926) periods.]

On back of some of the drawings, this imprinted admonition appears: "Not for sale. Salesman's use."

The typewritten letters and numbers, on the other hand, were made on an American machine of matching vintage and indicated which items were available and in what sizes.

The rubber-stamped codes 2675, A248, AA154, AA327, B899, UA44 and UA2716 were evidently affixed in Japan in accordance with instructions from, and paraphernalia supplied by, the manufacturer's U.S. representative or importer's agent, in all probability the Morimura brothers. These were production numbers or series numbers; very similar to our present day model codes or serial numbers.

The covered box scene (Example 3) also appears on plates, bowls, vases, ferners and sets of various types. Similarly, the vase in Example 4 is decorated with the same pattern obtainable on chocolate sets, cake sets and berry bowls, etc. The popular and familiar "Bedouin" scene (a.k.a. "Desert" scene and "Camel Rider" scene) is found not only on mugs, as shown in Example 5, but on a variety of other Nippon items as well.

The illustrations from which these photographs were made are the artist's original hand painted watercolor drawings. As might be expected, attention to detail was meticulous. Pencilled centerlines and outlines are visible. Some, such as Examples 3, 4 and 6 appear unfinished or incomplete because the artist purposely omitted irrelevant repetition and duplication.

In all four corners of Example 7 we were delighted to discover pencilled notations in the salesman's own handwriting!

Averaging 7½"x11½", each page was hand punched for easy insertion into, and removal from, a ring binder or loose-leaf type notebook. The sheets were later reinforced with tape (see Examples 1 and 5). As a result, the picture was sometimes partially obscured (as in Example 2). Some of the pages received so much wear and tear (popularity?), they had to be cropped or trimmed (Examples 6 and 7).

These illustrations and related material reached the United States and orders for merchandise, shipping instructions, etc., got to Japan aboard mail packets, cargo vessels and passenger ships. (As an outcome of Commodore Perry's visit to the Japanese Home Islands in 1853 and the Treaty of Kanagawa, commerce, trade and mail agreements had been promulgated in 1858).

The opening of the Panama Canal in 1914 radically shortened the Japan-to-New York voyage in much the same manner that the Suez Canal (1869) had reduced travel time between the Land of the Rising Sun and the Mediterranean, Europe and England.

Conducting business became progressively easier and faster as communication and transportation improvements followed one another in swift succession: extension of the trans-Pacific telegraph cable after 1905; a radio link in 1930; telephone service in 1934; Pan American's first "Clipper" flights in 1935. The last three of these developments, of course, occurred after the brief but glorious thirty-year span we all nostalgically refer to as "the Nippon era."

The thrill of discovering these drawings was further

---

*Including Woolworth's; mail-order giants such as Sears Roebuck and Montgomery-Ward; Larkin's famed Nippon premium "club" plan; Sperry-Hutchison Co. (S&H Green Stamps).

enhanced by the fact that two of them matched pieces already in our collection. Subsequently, we were able to pair up two others.

But the search and the fun go on. While we cannot prove, and do not claim, that these lovely watercolors are the long-sought after "master drawings," the dream of finding more drawings or sketches and the hunt for items that correspond to the remaining pictures has, for us, brought a whole new dimension to the passion of collecting Nippon.

We hope that our fellow Nippon fanciers find these beautiful paintings and the story behind them as interesting, as exciting and as pleasurable as we have.

Example 1. Canine pals adorn 10½″ molded-in-relief plaque.

Example 2. The "feel" and look of sapphire jewels on butterfly wings is simulated by a build-up of tempera bumps.

Example 3. Covered box 3½" x 4½" x 2⅛" (approximately). Upper: all-over lid decoration. Lower: Side detail (profile view).

Example 4. Vase 6¾". Water scenic, floral trim.

Example 5. Mug with familiar "Bedouin" scene. Tempera dots used to simulate look and "feel" of beading. Note similarity to Example 3.

Example 6. Vase, 9½″. "Framed" water scenic panel, floral trim.

Example 7. Plaque, 9½″. Salesman's pencilled notations visible at all four corners.

DINNERWARE PATTERNS

The first dinnerware pattern recorded by the Noritake Co. is that of the Sedan pattern. The company is also famous for its Gold and White, which is still being manufactured today and also for the Azalea pattern. Collectors wishing to know more about these particular patterns are advised to check *The Collector's Encyclopedia of Noritake* by Joan Van Patten for further information. This book shows numerous old ads for the Azalea pattern and extensive information about the Gold and White and Sedan.

The majority of Japanese dinnerware we find today was manufactured after the Nippon era. The pattern name is very often not marked on the Nippon-era pieces

and this presents a real problem to the owners who would like to match up their pieces.

I have been fortunate to locate a number of old Butler Bros. catalogs. Nine "Nippon" trademarked dinnerware sets were featured in them and are shown on the next few pages. These are all from the 1919-1920 period and surprisingly, I could find no other ads for Nippon dinnerware patterns in earlier editions. The nine shown are: Woodmere, Coronado, Danube, Wellington, Marseilles, Richelieu, Coronet, St. Regis and Blue and White. Hopefully, these old ads will help collectors and dealers identify their patterns.

From Butler Bros. catalog, 1919-1920 period

"ST. REGIS" PINK ENAMELED BORDER TRANSLUCENT CHINA (OPEN STOCK)

"Nippon" trademarked. Light wt. translucent china, first selection, extra fine white body, delicate pink rose and forget-me-not wreath border, enamel tracings, inner lt. green diamond motif design, all pieces with gold edges, all cups and hollow ware with heavy matt coin gold handles. An attractive pattern where quality counts. **No Package Charge.**

R1474—42 pc. set.
- 6 tea cups & saucers (12 pcs.)
- 12 plates, 6 each 7½ & 9⅞ in.
- 1 baker, 10½x7¾ in.
- 1 bowl, 5⅛x3⅛.
- 1 dish or platter, 10x7¼ in.
- 6 fruits, 5¼ in.
- 1 covd. sugar, ht. 4 in. (2 pcs.)
- 1 cream pitcher, ht. 3 in.
- 6 indiv. butters, 3¼ in.
- 1 set in carton, about 40 lbs.

SET (42 pcs.), **$15.50**

R1477—100A pc. set.
- 12 teas (24 pcs.)
- 36 plates, 6½, 7½ & 9⅞ in.
- 12 coupe soup plates, 7¼ in.
- 1 baker, 10½x7¾ in.
- 2 platters, 10x7¼ and 14x10¼ in.
- 12 fruits, 5¼ in.
- 1 sugar & creamer (3 pcs.)
- 1 butter, 7x4 in. (3 pcs.)
- 1 casserole, 10 in. (2 pcs.)
- 1 dish, 11¾x6⅞ in. (2 pcs.)
- 1 sauce boat, 9x3 in. (2 pcs.)
- 1 pickle dish, 8¼x4½ in.
- 1 set in bbl., about 90 lbs.

SET (100 pcs.), **$45.00**

R1476—100B pc. set. As 100A with 12 indiv. butters instead of 4 in. plates. 1 set in bbl., about 90 lbs.

SET (100 pcs.), **$43.65**

R1475—97 pc. set. As 100A without covd. butter (3 pcs.)

SET (97 pcs.), **$43.75**

From Butler Bros. catalog, 1919-1920 period

DINNERWARE IMPORTED CHINA

A choice showing of 42 and 100A pc. imported china dinner sets in open stock patterns. All light wt. clear translucent china, artistically decorated in various styles —neat conventional border designs, floral spray patterns, plain gold banded and all-over blue design. The shapes are also particularly pleasing. A prominent display of some of these sets will attract your most discriminating customers and bring you profitable sales. All first selection unless stated. NO PACKAGE CHARGE.

"WOODMERE" PINK FLORAL SPRAY TRANSLUCENT CHINA

"Nippon" trademarked. Light wt. translucent china. Large sprays of dainty pink wild flowers, green foliage background, wide gold edges, gold striped handles and knobs. A decoration that appeals. Stock this fast seller. It is priced low. **No Package Charge.**

R1024—42 pc. set.
- 6 tea cups 3½x2 & saucers 5½ in. (12 pcs.)
- 12 plates, 6 each 7½ & 8⅞ in.
- 1 baker, 10½x7¾ in.
- 1 bowl.
- 1 dish or platter, 11¾x8½ in.
- 6 fruits, 5⅓ in.
- 1 covd. sugar, ht. 4 in. (2 pcs.)
- 1 cream pitcher, ht. 3 in.
- 6 indv. butters.
- 1 set in carton, about 40 lbs.

SET (42 pcs.), **$12,75**

R1025—97 pc. set. As 100A without covd. butter (3 pcs.).
SET (97 pcs.), **$35.70**

R1026—100B pc. set. As 100A with 12 indiv. butters instead of 4 in. plates. 1 set in bbl., about 90 lbs.
SET (100 pcs.), **$35.50**

REQUEST Order open stock in not less than following quantities: 1 doz. 10c goods, ½ doz. 25c, ¼ doz. 50c

R1027—100A pc. set.
- 12 teas (24 pcs.)
- 36 plates, 6½, 7½ and 8⅞ in.
- 12 coupe soup plates, 7¼ in.
- 1 baker, 10½x7¾ in.
- 2 platters, 11¾x8½ and 14x10¼ in.
- 12 fruits, 5¼ in.
- 1 sugar & creamer, ht. 3 in. (3 pcs.)
- 1 butter, 7x4 (3 pcs.)
- 1 casserole, 10 in. (2 pcs.)
- 1 dish, 11¾x6⅞ in. (2 pcs.)
- 1 sauce boat, 9x3 in. (2 pcs.)
- 1 pickle dish, 8¼x4½ in.
- 1 set in bbl., about 90 lbs.

SET (100 pcs.), **$36.50**

"CORONADO" IVORY AND ROSE BORDER TRANSLUCENT CHINA

"Nippon" trademarked. Light wt. translucent china. American Beauty rose buds in wreath design, connecting stems, brown verge line, wide ivory border, gold edges and striped handles. A big value that deserves a most prominent place in your store. **No Package Charge.**

R1424—42 pc. set.
- 6 tea cups 3½x2 & saucers 5½ in. (12 pcs.)
- 12 plates, 6 each 7½ & 9⅞ in.
- 1 baker, 10½x7¾ in.
- 1 bowl, 5½ in.
- 1 dish or platter, 11¾x8½ in.
- 6 fruits, 5¼ in.
- 1 covd. sugar, ht. 4 in. (2 pcs.)
- 1 cream pitcher, ht. 3 in.
- 6 indv. butters, 3¼ in.
- 1 set in carton, about 40 lbs.

SET (42 pcs.), **$12.75**

R1425—97 pc. set. As 100A without covd. butter (3 pcs.)
SET (97 pcs.), **$35.70**

R1426—100B pc. set. As 100A with 12 indiv. butters instead of 4 in. plates. 1 set in bbl., about 90 lbs.
SET (100 pcs.), **$35.50**

NOTICE! Reduced output makes it necessary to limit orders for cups and saucers to 25% of any open stock pattern.

R1427—100A pc. set.
- 12 teas (24 pcs.)
- 36 plates, 8½, 7½ and 9⅞ in.
- 12 coupe soup plates, 7¼ in.
- 1 baker, 10½x7¾ in.
- 2 platters, 11¾x8½ and 14x10¼ in.
- 12 fruits, 5¼ in.
- 1 sugar creamer, ht. 3 in. (3 pcs.)
- 1 butter, 7x4 in. (3 pcs.)
- 1 casserole, 10 in. (2 pcs.)
- 1 dish, 11¾x6⅞ in. (2 pcs.)
- 1 sauce boat, 9x3 in. (2 pcs.)
- 1 pickle dish, 8¼x4½ in.
- 1 set in bbl., about 90 lbs.

SET (100 pcs.), **$36.50**

From Butler Bros. catalog, 1919-1920 period

"Danube" "Nippon" trademarked. Extra light wt., pure white translucent china, plain French shape, delft blue floral wreath scroll border, blue edges, hairline and inner hairline on shoulder, blue decorated handles.

For composition see table on right.

E30093—100A pc. set. 1 set about 90 lbs.
SET (100 pcs.), **$34.50**

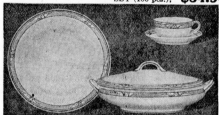

Wellington "Nippon" trademarked. Light wt., plain shape, translucent china, ⅜ in. ivory tinted band between tan verge lines, dainty pink rose spray medallions on shadow lattice background, gold decor. hdls. and edges. An unusually attractive decoration. **No Package Charge.**

For composition see table on right.

E30793—100A pc. set. 1 set about 90 lbs.
SET (100 pcs.), **$55.00**

"Marseilles," "Nippon" trademarked. Extra fine white body, dainty pink rose clusters between black enameled panels, inner gold verge line, gold edges.

For composition see table on right.

E30693—100A pc. set. 1 set about 90 lbs.
SET (100 pcs.), **$65.00**

COMPOSITION TABLE

OF DINNER SETS

IMPORTED AND DOMESTIC

Unless specified all our Imported and Domestic dinnerware sets conform to the following compositions. We will gladly furnish sets of any size or kind you may desire. Write for prices. We guarantee full sizes and full count. In figuring the number of pieces in asst. each SEPARATE PIECE counts as one, i. e.:

1 cup and 1 saucer	Count as	2 pcs.
1 cover, 1 butter and 1 drainer	"	3 "
1 cover, 1 sugar	"	2 "
1 cover, 1 dish or casserole	"	2 "
Sauce boat and stand	"	2 "

Dinner Sets comprise the following:	42 Pc. Set	50 Pc. Set	97 Pc. Set	100A Pc. Set	100B Pc. Set
Tea cup	6	6	12	12	12
Tea saucer	6	6	12	12	12
Bread & butter plate, 4 in.	—	6	12	12	—
Tea or pie plate....6 "	6	6	12	12	12
Dinner plate.......6 "	—	—	—	—	—
" " ....7 "	6	6	12	12	12
Coupe Soup.......6 "	—	6	12	12	12
Baker or vegetable dish.............7 "	1	1	1	1	1
Fancy bowl.......30's	1	1	—	—	—
Covd. butter & drainer...	—	—	—	1(3 pc)	1(3 pc)
Individual butter.......	6	—	—	—	12
Covd. casserole.....7 in.	—	—	1(2 pc)	1(2 pc)	1(2 pc)
Covd. dish.........7 "	—	1(2 pc)	1(2 pc)	1(2 pc)	1(2 pc)
Dish or platter......8 "	1	1	1	1	1
" " .....12 "	—	—	1	1	1
Fruit dish..........4 "	6	6	12	12	12
Pickle dish.	—	—	1	1	1
Sauce boat & stand......	—	—	1(2 pc)	1(2 pc)	1(2 pc)
Covd. sugar........30's	1(2 pc)	1(2 pc)	1(2 pc)	1(2 pc)	1(2 pc)
Cream pitcher.......30's	1	1	1	1	1
Approximate shipp'g wts.	40 lbs.	48 lbs.	80 lbs.	90 lbs.	90 lbs.

IMPORTANT—All makers' and jobbers' 42 and 100 pc. sets do not contain the same pieces. Be sure to compare the composition of the sets you buy. You may pay less, but you may also get smaller pieces. It is quite common now to make up skimpy dinnerware sets. Sizes specified above on individual pieces are trade sizes.

Richelieu "Nippon" trademarked. Light wt. translucent china, dainty pink rose spray border, scroll design in canary and peacock blue, gold edges and half matt handles. Something extremely attractive, decidedly new—"Frenchy" in appearance.

For composition see table on left.

E31193—100A pc. set.—1 set about 90 lbs.
SET (100 pcs.), **$72.00**

Coronet, "Nippon" trademarked. Extra fine light wt. translucent china, plain shape, wide burnished coin gold edges and inner verge line, half matt gold handles and knobs, gold base line on upright pcs.

For composition see table on left.

E31393—100A pc. set. 1 set about 90 lbs.
SET (100 pcs.), **$95.00**

From Butler Bros. catalog, 1919-1920 period

GEISHA GIRL PORCELAIN OF THE NIPPON ERA

by Elyce Litts

Among the myriad of designs found on Nippon porcelain, there exists a group of wares called Geisha Girl Porcelain which features kimono-clad ladies and children in scenes of everyday pre-modern Japanese life. The study of Geisha Girl patterns is a study of the history and culture of Japan itself -- from the Basket pattern depicting the gathering of cockle-shells to the Tea House patterns showing the Japanese tea ceremony (chanoyu) to the Temple pattern exhibiting the magnificent layout of the native Shinto religious grounds. The variety of scenes to be found on Geisha ware is truly incredible, and additional ones are still coming to light. The 175 plus patterns and over 100 manufacturer's and artisan's marks currently catalogued attest to Geisha Girl Porcelain's widespread popularity over the years.

Unlike many of its Nippon counterparts, Geisha ware retained an Oriental motif while bowing to the export market in terms of function and style. These busy, colorful wares were produced in the same table and utility pieces as other Nippon items. Examples ranging from tea and cocoa sets to ashtrays, doll's items and miniatures were produced. One can collect a single border color, a single pattern or fill an entire shelf with differently shaped and designed cups and saucers. The most commonly found forms are tea wares (except caddies), salt and pepper sets, small bowls, and bread and butter plates. The rarer items include large plates and platters, mugs, candlesticks, miniatures, and complete sets. The author has yet to come across a non-reproduction tumbler, and has heard of only one mustache cup.

Geisha Girl patterns were either wholly handpainted, handpainted over a stencilled design, or, infrequently, comprised of a decal. An entire scene might encompass the porcelain body or several scenes in reserves might sit on a diaper patterned ground. Old catalogues describe these scenes in a variety of ways: "Japanese figures and landscapes", "Geisha dancers", "Japanese girls and landscape", "Japanese figure, flower and lantern decoration", etc. Collectors have given all these patterns descriptive names as a means of identification. There are at least 30 patterns and variations thereof known to have been produced during the Nippon era. These include:

Bridge Talk	Flower Gathering series
Butterfly	Flute and Koto
Carp	Garden Bench series
Child Wearing E-boshi	Geisha in Cards
Circle Dance	Geisha in Sampan series
Doll's Tea Party	Greeting Grandma
Feather Fan	Inside the Tea House
Lantern	Reaching for Butterfly
Leaving the Tea House	Rivers Edge Variations
Mother & Son	Servant with Sack
Parasol series	Temple
Pointing series	Torii
Porch	Waterboy

Each Geisha Girl item is bordered by one or a combination of the following colors: a variety of red, blue or green hues, rhubarb, maroon, yellow, brown or gold. Red-orange is, by far, the most commonly found. These colors may be applied in bands, scallops or waves around the perimeters of body and lid as well as on spouts, handles and finials. Borders are often embellished by gold or enamel flowers, lacing or geometrics, and sometimes there is even an interior border of flowers, butterflies or gold. Butler Bros. catalogues from the first decade of this century variously describe borders as: "gold traced cobalt edges", "Tokio red bands and handles", "gold ornamented pale green edge", "floral wreath framing, gold ornamented Tokio red edge", "red and green Oriental border".

Among the Nippon marks found on Geisha Girl Porcelain are:

C.O.N. In Diamond	Pagoda
Crown (Made in Nippon)	Paulownia
Green M in Wreath	Royal Kaga
Maple Leaf	SH
Made in (Nippon)	SNB Nagoya
Nagoya Shofu	TE-OH China
NIPPON	Torii
Nippon with ideograph	TN in Wreath
Noritake Nippon	WPSK (Powsie Coture)
T&Z New York (importer's trademark)	

It is apparent from the marking/pattern combinations that much of the Geisha ware was completed in decorating centers which bought porcelain blanks from the major kilns. For instance, a master berry bowl in the Geisha in Sampan pattern was bottom stamped Torii Nippon while the matching individual bowls were signed Kutani. The Geisha Girl Temple pattern can be found with six different marks including the M in Wreath, Tree Crest and Royal Kaga Nippon marks. See Example 1.

What of unmarked items? Geisha Girl production continued past the Nippon period and, while the number of extant examples marked Japan far outnumbers those marked Nippon, the number of unmarked and idiograph marked items is greater still. It seems plausible that many of the Nippon-period Geisha Girl pieces were not marked. Geisha ware was often sold in open stock and, as has been indicated, importation laws allowed for the marking of the crate or case rather than the individual items contained therein. Even for those items sold as a set, the laws allowed for only one member of the set to be marked. The point is to be aware that, marked or not, there is documented proof that many of the Geisha Girl patterns were produced during the Nippon era.

Among the Nippon Geisha Girl items of greatest interest are those used for advertising purposes. The pictured "Doll's Tea Party" patterned cup exhibits a date of 1916 and the saucer bears the "NIPPON" bottomstamp (Example 2). Emery, Birel, Thayer & Co. was a large Kansas City department store. Every year between 1915 and 1953, they held a Doll's Tea Party for all their young shoppers. Little girls brought their favorite dolls to be judged for originality, costume, most distant origin, etc. Each participant received a cup and saucer as a gift. While no company documents are in existence, it is possible that these dated cups were the prizes. As depicted on the saucer, Hahne & Co. also took the opportunity to influence the young shopper to bring Mom back to their store; its accompanying cup bears only the Geisha Girl pattern.

Another interesting story is brought to us in the guise of the diminutive teapot in Example 3. It is bottom stamped "Cafe Martin, New York". The cafe opened in 1899 and was closed down during Prohibition in 1920, i.e., it operated during the Nippon era. Its founder, Louis Martin, was noted as an innovator for the introduction of Art Nouveau styling to an American cafe and for allowing women into a drinking establishment! No doubt these charming little teapots were used to entice the female clientele. Also available to customers were decorative little tin boxes of French mints. The discreet lady would not want to come home with the smell of liquor on her breath!

Because of its widespread and continuing popularity, Geisha Girl Porcelain is still being produced. New items include tumblers, tea sets, usually Chinese style with bamboo pot handle and handle-less cups, sake sets, plates, vases, toothbrush holders, toothpick holders, dresser sets and children's demitasse cups.

Reproductions are recognizable by the following characteristics:

1. Porcelain color and appearance: repros are of smooth white porcelain; older wares tend to be gray and coarse.

2. Color finish: repros tend to have less applied enamel and color washes.

3. Border color: most repros have a red-orange border.

4. Appearance of Geisha: reproduction Geisha tend to have pointy noses at angles peculiar to their faces.

5. Use of gold: repros rarely have gold as a part of the scenic decoration and have minimal, if any, gold decoration on the border. New gold will gleam while old gold will show tarnish.

6. Structural design: like the decoration, the structural design of repros is generally simple -- plain rounded shapes, few scallops or fancy curves. Repros will always have molded parts, while many of the older items exhibit some hand formation.

7. Marks: It is known that some current reproductions display a "Double T-in-Diamond, Made in Japan" mark. Others have a mark in Japanese indicating the importer's name. To date, none have come to light with any of the fake Nippon marks.

Prices for Geisha Girl porcelain are comparable to similar examples of other Nippon pieces.

Example 1, Geisha Girl. Demitasse cup and saucer, Temple pattern, multi-color border. Saucer is signed Kutani; cup bears green M in wreath mark.

Example 2, Geisha Girl. Doll's Tea Party pattern cup and saucer, apple green border. Cup stands 2¼"
tall.

Example 3, Geisha Girl. Cafe Martin teapot, 2½" tall, Geisha in Cards pattern, cobalt blue border with gold lacing.

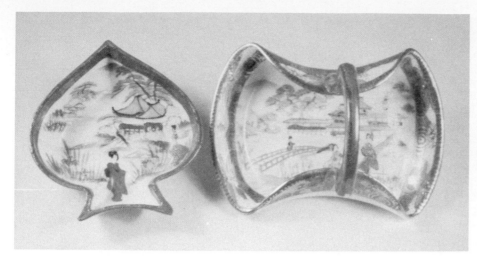

Left: Ashtray from bridge set, 3″, Temple pattern, green M in wreath mark. Right: Basket, 2¼″ x 3¾″, Temple pattern, green M in wreath mark.

Tea set, 5″ pot, creamer, sugar, 3 cup and saucers, Rivers Edge pattern, SNB Nagoya mark.

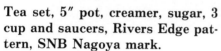

Pedestaled salt, 1½″, Temple pattern, Noritake Tree Crest mark.

Left: Trinket box, 2″ tall, Temple pattern, Royal Kaga mark. Right: Hatpin holder, 5″ tall, Temple pattern, green M in wreath mark.

Relish, 10″, Parasol pattern, green M in wreath mark.

Sugar bowl, 6″, Feather Fan pattern, Royal Kaga mark.

Trivet, 6″, Feather Fan pattern, Royal Kaga mark.

Saucer, 4¾″, Torii pattern, TN in wreath mark.

PHOENIX BIRD CHINAWARE

by Joan Collett Oates

It is hard to believe that Phoenix Bird chinaware has been in existence for over 70 years. In fact, just a few years from now the pattern will be a genuine antique. Many of these pieces were listed and pictured in a 1914 A. A. Vantine & Co. catalog from New York City and Phoenix Bird is just as popular today as it was back then, more so probably because of today's antique trade papers that have carried articles about the pattern in the last few years.

Here is a pattern that can be as simple or as complex as a collector wants it to be. It all depends upon the collector's complacency toward his or her pieces and perhaps the weight of one's wallet. One can be satisfied with having a simple set of tea or breakfast dishes or one can not be content until each and every one of the shapes, forms (plain and scalloped-edged), marks, shades of blue and minor differences are in his collection. All of these variances add up to over 400 pieces! And quite a number of dollars to say the least.

In its infancy (circa 1914), it was introduced as HOWO CHINAWARE; in 1919 it was BLUE & WHITE HOWO BIRD CHINA DINNERWARE; in 1920 as simply HOWO BIRD; and in 1922, by Charles William Stores, N.Y., as BLUE HOWO BIRD CHINA, "a uniquely different set in blue underglaze, all over decoration of Japanese Bird of Paradise, known as the famous Howo Bird decoration." Butler Bros., in the 1919-20 era, noted it as "Translucent white china, Howo bird and scroll decoration in two color Oriental blue. Very popular ware - always sells big." The dishes came "NIPPON" trademarked up until Butler's Spring, 1921 advertisement; after that it was only listed as being "Trademarked." Which one of the 80 different marks cataloged could that trademark have been? Of several possibilities, the most likely are those having an M in wreath motif and/or crossed stems or maybe just Made in Japan.

For many years the pattern seemed to lose favor with its owners and was often left behind to be included in the sale of their cottage when it was sold. As the pattern began to emerge once again, it somehow, somewhere, acquired two names, Phoenix Bird and Flying Turkey. As research began, several phoenix patterns began to surface and soon it became apparent that each of them needed a formal name. The Flying Turkey title was applied to one whose background was quite similar to the Phoenix Bird but not having the same border or bird design. And the Flying Turkey has now become a pattern in its own right! Until they began to note the diffences, collectors mixed the patterns, unknowingly, because oftentimes, the shades of blue did match each other. Today, however, these pieces are now very often found in separate cupboards, each pattern being very "collectible" but, sorry to say, not always "affordable."

Finding a piece of Phoenix Bird with the backstamp, NIPPON, means only one thing . . . that it was manufactured during the period of 1891-1921. It does not guarantee that a piece is of fine grade china nor that it is of poor grade. Also, it does not guarantee that it will be of a particular shade of blue, a spectacular grade of print or that the design will be identical to another piece of Phoenix Bird having the same shade of blue, grade of print or having the same backstamp. A piece may or may not have any one of the above characteristics and be from the Nippon era and/or beyond. In reality it is a confusing collectible as well as a frustrating one, to say the least . . . the pattern varies in so many respects.

Some of the plates from the Nippon era have much more cobalt blue than others, for example the plate in Example 1. These sometimes also have a larger than usual flower. In Example 2, the softer shade of blue is evident in the cereal bowl on the left and it also has a better grade of print. In other words, one example of a "Nippon"-marked piece of Phoenix bird will not be as good as, or as poor as, another. This is true also of whatever the backstamp a piece carries. The majoriy of pieces must be judged on their individual merits.

In early catalogs by A. A. Vantine & Co., N.Y.C., (1914 and 1916), the following is found "Howo Chinaware is Japanese ware, pleasing in design and very serviceable. Ever since Chinaware has been known, its dainty color scheme of blue and white has been much admired. By applications of modern science, it has been made particularly strong and durable, and is therefore suited to everyday use." It is impossible to know which of the backstamps was used in the teapot shown in the Vantine catalogs but an item identical in shape in this author's collection has the backstamp of a concave M under two crossed stems, each stem has a few leaves and under this is JAPAN. This is said to be one of the marks of the Morimura Brothers, affiliated with Noritake.

Phoenix Bird chinaware, in selected pieces, was also offered now and then as a premium, sometimes as a breakfast set and sometimes packed in packages of tea and/or coffee by Montgomery Ward and by A. J. Kasper, Importers of Chicago. The pattern was also made in child-size pieces (not doll-size) for the little lady of the house. It is a small wonder that some of the eggshell ovoid shaped cups and saucers ever survived the hands of little children! There are also 5" plates, small

60

teapots, creamers and sugars, small covered tureens, a handled cake plate (just like mother's); however, it is the ovoid cups and their matching saucers shown on the left in Example 3, which have the word Nippon on the base, but only on the saucers. The saxon shaped cups and saucers shown on the right in Example 3 are not as "pretty" or as thin as the former. To date, about 26 different sized cups have been found in this pattern.

The Nippon-marked chocolate shown in Example 4 is exceptional in quality as well as print. Note the shade of blue as well as the amount of design. Both are unusual. There are cups and saucers to match but they carry no backstamp. Collectors will note that the border is different than the traditional one and Phoenix Bird having this variance are identified as HO-O.

The sugar and the creamer shown in Example 5 are round and fat and have a large C-type handle which has a bamboo ridge on it although not all creamers and sugars in this pattern have this trait. This particular set comes in two sizes, medium small and large. They are the same shape as shown in the 1919 Butler Bros. advertisement and in a few following it. Whether or not the items listed were marked Nippon, or should have been, the two sets in this collector's cupboard are not! Neither creamer is marked, one sugar has only Japan, and the other has Japanese idiographs.

Besides being sold by Butler Bros., A. A. Vantine, Charles Williams Stores and F. W. Woolworth's Five and Tens, Phoenix Bird was offered as a gift by *Needlecraft Magazine* if one sold a certain number of subscriptions. These were advertised as "not being 'seconds' sometimes sold in the cut-rate stores but the best selected pieces - a set to be proud of."

All good things eventually got copied and so did the Phoenix Bird. Around 1936, an English firm, Myott & Son, also produced the pattern. These wares were however not of porcelain but of earthenware and their shapes were not the same as those made by Japanese factories but more of an English nature.

Prices for Phoenix Bird Chinaware are comparable to similar examples of other Nippon pieces.

Chamberstick, 2″ tall, "saucer" is 5″ across.

Individual teapot, 3¼″ tall.

Butter tub and drain.

Selection of mustard pots in Phoenix Bird pattern.

Set, sugar is 5¾″ wide, creamer is 4¾″ wide.

Creamer and sugar set; note that creamer has its own cover.

The gravy boat is 7¾″ long and the attached plate is 8½″ long. The pattern is the Twin Phoenix; the mark is Royal Sometuke Nippon.

The mustard pot has an attached saucer which is 4½″ in diameter. The pot is 3″ tall including the cover. The bell-shaped salt and pepper shakers are 2¾″ tall. These items are decorated in the Twin Phoenix pattern and bear the Royal Sometuke mark.

Example 1, Phoenix Bird plate.

Example 4, Phoenix Bird chocolate pot.

Example 2, Phoenix Bird bowls.

Example 3, Phoenix Bird cups and saucers.

Example 5, Phoenix Bird sugar and creamer.

Sugar and creamer set, mark #189; eggcup, mark #191.

Saucer, on left, bread and butter plate, 6″ in diameter, on right. Both have mark #55.

Chocolate cup and saucer, mark #55.

Plate 9. Gravy boat, mark #55.

Shortcake dishes, 7⅜″ in diameter, mark #189.

OTHER TYPES OF NIPPON

Although Nippon collectors tend to collect ONLY porcelain items, Nippon pieces, in fact, can be any item manufactured in Japan between the years of 1891 and 1921 and backstamped with the country of origin, Nippon. This includes basketware, pottery pieces, anything and everything. Many collectors have attempted to add some of these other types of Nippon-era wares to their collections and I personally feel that they can be a nice addition. This book deals exclusively with the collectible porcelain pieces but in an attempt to introduce some of these other wares to collectors, I have included photos of a pair of wooden candlesticks and two types of pottery-type vases. Since very little research has been done on these wares, I would caution collectors to buy with an eye toward quality and to purchase only those items which really enhance their porcelain collection.

The candlesticks are incised Nippon and also bear a paper label saying Made in Miyajima Japan. The green vase is 9½" tall, bears the green M in wreath mark and is a combination of cloisonné and pottery decor. The other vase is 6" tall, incised with the word NIPPON and is very different from our porcelain wares.

Pair of wooden candlesticks.

Close-up of paper label on candlestick.

Pottery vase.

Pottery vase.

REPRODUCTION ALERT

Whenever an item becomes popular with the public, and especially when the prices begin to soar, there are bound to be reproductions made of it. However, most of the so-called Nippon reproductions don't even resemble the Nippon-era wares but there is a "Nippon" backstamp found on them and many collectors and dealers have been fooled by these reproductions.

There are now thousands and thousands of these items on the market and just as soon as most collectors become aware of one pattern the manufacturers design other styles, patterns and backstamps.

Unfortunately, these items are quite legal. They are currently manufactured in Japan with a "Nippon" mark of some type under the glaze and along with this a small paper label is affixed to the bottom saying "Made in Japan". Dealers buy in wholesale amounts from the importing firms. First to get discarded are the little boxes the items are originally packed in and then the paper label saying Japan comes off, and voila, a genuine "Nippon" marked article appears. There is presently nothing collectors can do about this situation due to the current status of our import laws and the way they are written. So, a word of advice: either know what you are buying or know who you are buying from. And also keep in mind that many honest dealers who do not handle a lot of Nippon may also have purchased some of these items without knowing that they were reproduction pieces. Give them the benefit of the doubt. BUT if you find these items in great abundance at any one dealer's shop or booth at a show and they are not marked as reproductions, RUN, don't walk from this person!

The pattern found most with the biggest variety of pieces is the "wildflower". These items have a bisque finish and the outside edges of each piece are highlighted with gold and have pink-to-lavender flower blossoms as the decoration. All wares in this pattern bear the bogus hourglass in a wreath mark.

Another pattern collectors should be aware of is the one called "green mist" by the importer. These items also have a bisque finish with a light-to-medium green background. Pink flowers and gold trim decorate the wares. The items are reminiscent of Limoges items in shape. The mark found on these pieces is similar to the familiar Nippon rising sun mark except that the rays are a little different than the genuine one.

"Antique rose" is one of the newest patterns collectors are finding. There are a variety of items to be found in this pattern and collectors would be smart to study the pattern and the sketches of available pieces which follow. Items in this pattern bear the bogus maple leaf mark which is an almost duplicate of the genuine mark except that it is much larger in size. The actual leaf in the bogus mark is about ½" long compared to the ¼" size of the real one.

Collectors should also beware of the reproduction tea set consisting of a teapot, sugar bowl, creamer and six small cups and saucers which have a glossy white background. The design consists of pink and red roses. In my opinion, it is one of the few reproduction items that does resemble genuine Nippon pieces. However, the gold trim is more of a luster type than that found on genuine wares. These items are also backstamped with the large maple leaf mark. Another pattern found with this backstamp is the "orchid" tea set consisting of a teapot, sugar bowl and creamer. These pieces have a yellow background with orchid flowers as the decoration.

"Texas rose" is another design for which to be on the lookout. To date, researchers have found an ewer, night set, milk pitcher, cup and saucer and tea set in this pattern. The pattern comes in two different colorings, both have a light green background, however, one has pink and red flowers, the other has gold and light brown flowers. All of these pieces have been backstamped with the bogus rising sun mark.

Collectors will also find another tea set available which consists of a teapot, creamer, sugar bowl and four cups and saucers. The pattern is pink and lavender flowers on a white bisque background. The bogus rising sun mark is found on these wares.

Last, but not least collectors have reported finding reproduction pieces in the "dogwood" pattern. To date they have spotted a cracker jar, covered box and a hat-pin holder. No other information or photos are available on these except that the items are backstamped with the large maple leaf mark.

Collectors should get the "feel" of genuine pieces as well as learn what the bogus marks and patterns are. Don't end up paying Nippon prices for reproduction wares!

MARKS FOUND ON REPRODUCTION WARES

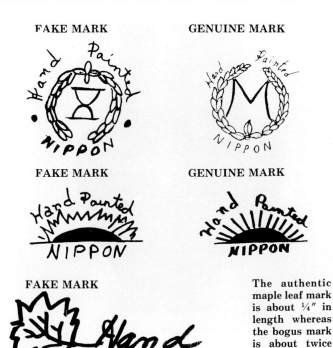

FAKE MARK   GENUINE MARK

FAKE MARK   GENUINE MARK

FAKE MARK

The authentic maple leaf mark is about ¼" in length whereas the bogus mark is about twice the size or about ½" long.

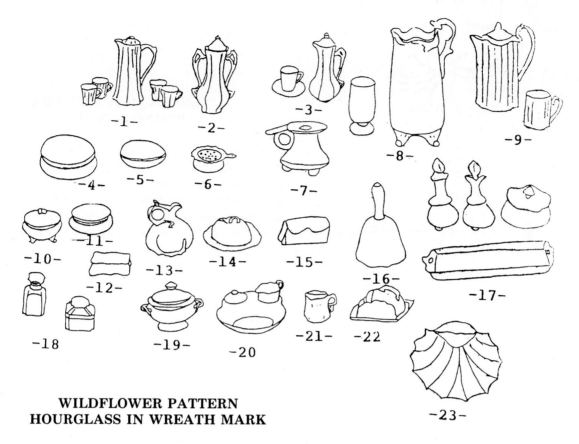

WILDFLOWER PATTERN
HOURGLASS IN WREATH MARK

1. Mocha set, pot is 11″ tall, comes with four matching cups
2. Urn, 12″ tall
3. Chocolate set, pot is 10″ tall, four cups and saucers
4. Large dresser jar, 7″ across
5. Egg box, 5⅜″ across
6. Tea strainer and receptacle, strainer is 5″ across
7. Portable candlestick, 4″ tall
8. Lemonade set, pitcher is 14¾″ tall, four tumblers, 5½″ tall
9. Mocha set, pitcher is 8½″ tall, comes with four cups
10. Footed box, 4⅞″ wide
11. Hinged powder box, 5¾″ across
12. Trinket box, 5¾″ across
13. Ewer, 8″ tall
14. Butter dish, melon shape, 7½″ wide
15. Letter valet, 7½″ wide
16. Bell, 5⅛″ tall
17. Dresser set, tray is 10¼″ long, perfume bottles are 6″ tall
18. Dresser set, 5″ cologne bottle, 3½″ powder jar
19. Lidded sauce tureen, 7¾″ across
20. Berry set, tray is 7½″ wide, comes with creamer and sugar lid
21. Mustache cup, 3½″ tall
22. Slanted cheese dish, 8¾″ long
23. Shell dish, 6″ across

GREEN MIST PATTERN
RISING SUN MARK

24. Sugar, 5½" across, creamer, 4" across
25. Powder box, 4⅛" across
26. Master sugar bowl, 6⅛" tall
27. Crimped sugar bowl, 5½" across
28. Tea set, teapot is 7¼" tall, sugar bowl and creamer

ANTIQUE ROSE PATTERN
MAPLE LEAF MARK

29. Creamer and sugar bowl, creamer is 5⅝" wide
30. Cream pitcher, 6¾" tall
31. Cream pitcher, 5¼" tall
32. Night set, 7" tall, set consists of glass and water container
33. Salt and pepper set, each is 2¾" tall
34. Flask vase, 6" tall
35. Bell, 4⅛" tall
36. Master pitcher or tankard, 11½" tall
37. Mug, 4¾" tall, together with the master pitcher is being sold as a Nippon tankard set

-38- -39- -40-

-41- -42-

TEXAS ROSE PATTERN
RISING SUN MARK

38. Night set, 7″ tall when glass is mounted on top
39. Ewer, 8″ tall
40. Cream pitcher, 6¾″ tall
41. Cup and saucer, cup is 3⅝″ tall
42. Tea set, pot is 6″ tall, creamer and sugar bowl

-43-

ORCHID PATTERN
MAPLE LEAF MARK

43. Tea set, teapot is 7½″ tall, sugar bowl and creamer

-44-

-45-

PATTERN NAMES UNKNOWN

44. Tea set, teapot is 7½″ tall, sugar bowl, creamer, six
    cups and saucers; maple leaf mark
45. Teapot, 7½″ tall, part of a tea set including creamer,
    sugar bowl, four cups and saucers; rising sun mark

WILDFLOWER REPRODUCTION

GREEN MIST REPRODUCTION

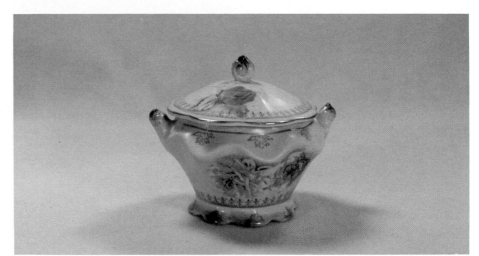

ANTIQUE ROSE REPRODUCTION

ORCHID REPRODUCTION

REPRODUCTION - PATTERN UNKNOWN

REPRODUCTIONS - PATTERN NAME UNKNOWN

TEXAS ROSE REPRODUCTIONS

NIPPON PHOTO TIPS

by George Murphy

Taking good, clear photos of Nippon wares often poses a problem to both collectors and dealers. As an aid to amateur photographers, the following information is offered:

CAMERA: Use a single lens reflex camera. If you use a pocket camera, Instamatic, Polaroid, Disc camera, etc., you can expect pictures that are out of focus, fuzzy and off-center, because snapshot type cameras are not suited to close-up work.

LIGHTING: Light your subject with photoflood lamps. Electronic flash and flashbulb lighting is too flat and produces unwanted shadows and reflections. Sunlight is too harsh.

FILM: With photoflood lighting use Kodak Ektachrome 160 Tungsten film for slides. For negatives use Kodacolor with an 80A filter on the lens to balance it to photoflood lighting.

MORE LIGHTING: You'll need two ECA-250w. photoflood lamps in aluminum reflectors, with plastic clip-on diffuser discs to soften shadows. Lightweight telescoping light stands will provide the flexibility you need in trying various lighting positions.

ACCESSORIES: A camera tripod is a must to allow precise focusing, framing and centering. Always use a lens hood when working close to strong lighting. A set of lens extension rings will allow you to focus close to your subject using your normal standard 50mm lens.

BACKGROUNDS: Use plain backgrounds of colored construction paper or Bristol board. Don't use fabric - the inevitable folds and creases will show up. Don't use stark black or white backgrounds. Besides being campy, black or white backgrounds may tend to mislead your exposure meter. Curve the background to eliminate a "horizon" line.

MORE LIGHTING: Start by placing your lights on either side of, and higher than, the camera and aiming them at the subject at about a 45° angle to the lens axis. Experiment with different lighting locations until your viewfinder shows an image that is evenly lighted and has a minimum of distracting shadows and reflections.

EXPOSURE: Set your camera's automatic metering or exposure system at f/11 - f/16. If your subject is very light or very dark, refer to your camera's instruction manual for intentional over-or-under exposure. To avoid camera movement, use a cable release or your camera's self-timer to release the shutter.

MORE LIGHTING: Photography has been defined as the Art of Painting with Light, so if you are getting the impression that lighting is important, you are correct. In fact, the next entire section is devoted to lighting.

STANDARD LIGHTING SETUP

* Subject on a curved background taped to a carton or wall.

* Camera with lens hood, mounted on a tripod.

* The lamps get hot. To keep cool and to prolong lamp life, use a dimmer. Turn lamps up full only for the actual exposure.

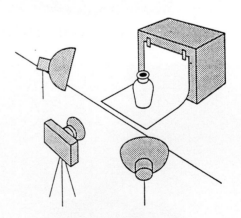

BOUNCE LIGHTING SETUP

* Eliminates shadows and "hot spot" reflections of the lights off glazed surfaces.

* Each bounce reflector should be flat white, such as white card or a pillow case pulled over a box.

* Position the lights and bounce reflectors so that each reflector prevents the light from one lamp from hitting the subject directly, and at the same time reflects the light from the other lamp onto the subject and the background.

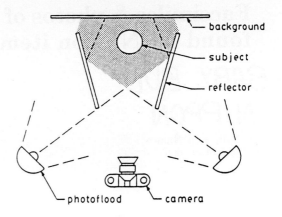

DIMMER

Shown is a simple combination dimmer and extension cord you can build yourself from easily obtained components. The diode is a 200 PIV 3 amp. rectifier. The line cord should be able 12′ long, with a strain relief bushing where it passes through the box.

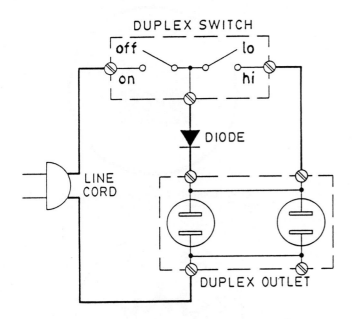

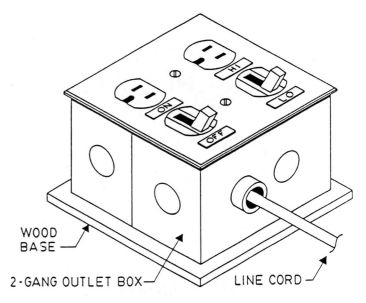

Facsimiles & photos of marks found on Nippon items

BABY BUD NIPPON

1. Baby Bud Nippon incised on doll

BARA
HAND PAINTED
CO
L
NIPPON

2. Bara hand painted Nippon

3. Carpathia M Nippon

4. Cherry blossom hand painted Nippon found in blue, green & magenta colors

5. Cherry blossom in a circle hand painted Nippon

6. Chikusa hand painted Nippon

7. China E-OH hand painted Nippon found in blue & green colors

8. Crown (pointed), hand painted Nippon found in green & blue colors

9. Crown Nippon (pointed). Made in Nippon found in green and blue colors

10. Crown (square), hand painted Nippon found in green and green with red colors

11. Chubby LW & Co. Nippon
found on dolls

15. Double T Diamond in circle Nippon

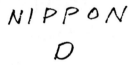

12. D Nippon

16. Dowsie Nippon

13. Dolly sticker found on Nippon's Dolly dolls,
sold by Morimura Bros.

17. EE Nippon

14. Double T Diamond, Nippon

18. Elite B hand painted Nippon

19. FY 401 Nippon
found on dolls

23. Hand painted Nippon

FY

NIPPON
405

20. FY 405 Nippon
found on dolls

Hand Painted

Nippon

24. Hand painted Nippon

21. G in a circle
hand painted Nippon

HAND PAINTED

NIPPON

25. Hand painted Nippon

Hand Painted

NIPPON

26. Hand painted Nippon

22. Gloria L.W. & Co. hand painted
Nippon (Louis Wolf Co., Boston, Mass. & N.Y.C.)

Handpainted

NIPPON

27. Hand painted Nippon

28. Hand painted Nippon with symbol

33. Hand painted Nippon with symbol

29. Hand painted Nippon with symbol

30. Hand painted Nippon with symbol

34. Hand painted Nippon with symbol

31. Hand painted Nippon with symbol

35. Hand painted Nippon with symbol

32. Hand painted Nippon with symbol

36. Horsman No. 1 Nippon
found on dolls

37. IC Nippon

38. Imperial Nippon
found in blue & green

39. JMDS Nippon

40. Jonroth Studio hand painted Nippon

41. Kid Doll M.W. & Co. Nippon

42. Kinjo Nippon

43. Kinjo China hand painted Nippon

44. L & Co. Nippon

45. LFH hand painted Nippon

46. LW & Co. Nippon (Louis Wolf & Co.,
Boston, Mass & N.Y.C.)

50. M M hand painted Nippon

47. M in wreath, hand painted Nippon
(M stands for importer, Morimura Bros.)
found in green, blue, magenta & gold colors

51. Made in Nippon

52. Maple leaf Nippon found in green, blue & magenta

48. M. in wreath hand painted Nippon, D.M. Read Co.
(M stands for importer, Morimura Bros.)

49. M B (Morimura Bros.)
Baby Darling sticker
found on dolls

53. Morimura Bros.
sticker found on Nippon items

54. Mt. Fujiyama Nippon

NIPPON

55. Nippon
found in blue, gold and also incised into items

NIPPON 84

56. Nippon 84

NIPPON 144

57. Nippon 144

*221
NIPPON*

58. Nippon 221

59. Nippon with symbol

60. Nippon with symbol

61. Nippon with symbol

NIPPON

62. Nippon with symbol

63. Nippon with symbol

64. Nippon with symbol

65. Nippon M incised on doll
(note N is written backwards)
#12 denotes size of doll
M = Morimura Bros.

70. Oriental china Nippon

66. Noritake M in wreath Nippon
M = Morimura Bros.
found in green, blue & magenta

71. Pagoda hand painted Nippon

67. Noritake Nippon
found in green, blue & magenta colors

PATENT
NO 30441
NIPPON

72. Patent #30441 Nippon

NORITAKE
NIPPON

68. Noritake Nippon
found in green, blue & magenta colors

73. Paulownia flowers & leaves
hand painted Nippon (crest used by
Empress of Japan, kiri no mon)
found in a green/red color

69. OAC Hand painted Nippon
(Okura Art China, branch of Noritake Co.)

74. Paulownia flowers & leaves
hand painted Nippon (crest
used by Empress of Japan, kiri no mon)

75. Pickard etched china, Noritake Nippon
Pickard mark is in black
Noritake/Nippon mark is blue in color

78. Queue San Baby Sticker
found on Nippon dolls

79. RC Nippon

76. Pickard hand painted china Nippon

80. RC hand painted Nippon
combination of both red & green colors

81. RC Noritake Nippon hand painted
found in green & blue

77. Pickard hand-painted china, Noritake Nippon
Pickard mark printed in black
Noritake Nippon in magenta

82. RC Noritake Nippon

83. RE Nippon

84. Rising Sun Nippon

85. Royal Dragon Nippon

86. Royal Dragon Nippon
Studio hand painted

87. Royal Kaga Nippon

88. Royal Kinran Nippon
found in blue, gold colors

89. Royal Kinran Crown Nippon
found in blue, gold & green colors

90. Royal Moriye Nippon
found in green & blue colors

91. Royal Nishiki Nippon

92. Royal Satsuma Nippon
(cross within a ring, crest of House of Satsuma)

93. Royal Sometuke Nippon

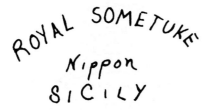

94. Royal Sometuke Nippon Sicily

95. R.S. Nippon

96. S & K hand painted Nippon
found in green, blue & magenta colors

97. S & K hand painted Nippon
found in green, blue & magenta colors

98. Shinzo Nippon

99. Shofu Nagoya Nippon

100. SNB Nippon

104. Studio hand painted Nippon

101. SNB Nagoya Nippon

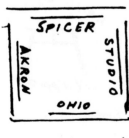

102. Spicer Studio Akron Ohio Nippon

105. Superior hand painted Nippon

103. Spoke hand painted Nippon

106. T Nippon
(2 ho·o birds)

107. T hand painted Nippon

111. TS hand painted Nippon

108. T in wreath hand painted Nippon

112. Teacup Nippon

109. T N hand painted Nippon
mark is red & green

113. Torii Nippon

110. TS hand painted Nippon

114. Tree crest Nippon
(crest of Morimura family)

117. Yamato hand painted Nippon

115. Tree Crest & Maple leaf hand painted Nippon

118. Yamato Nippon

116. V Nippon, Scranton, Pa.

119. C.G.N. Hand painted Nippon
found in green

120. F Nippon
03601
600 found incised on dolls

121. F. Nippon
#76012
601 found incised on dolls

NO. 76018
NIPPON
30/3

122. F. Nippon
#76018 30/3
found incised on dolls

No. 76018
NIPPON
403

123. F. Nippon
#76018
403

FY
NIPPON

124. FY Nippon
found incised on dolls

FY
NIPPON
301

125. FY Nippon 301
found incised on dolls

FY
NIPPON
402

126. FY Nippon 402
found incised on dolls.

FY 9
NIPPON
402

127. FY 9 Nippon 402
found incised on dolls

FY
NIPPON
404

128. FY Nippon 404
found incised on dolls

FY
NIPPON
406

129. FY Nippon 406
found incised on dolls

FY
NIPPON
464

130. FY Nippon 464
found incised on dolls

131. FY Nippon
#17604 604
found incised on dolls

132. FY Nippon
#70018 004
found incised on dolls

133. FY Nippon (variation of mark)
#70018 403 found incised on dolls

134. FY Nippon
#70018 406
found incised on dolls

135. FY Nippon (variation of mark)
#70018 406
found incised on dolls

136. FY Nippon
76018
found incised on dolls.

137. Jollikid sticker
(red & white)
found on dolls

138. Ladykin sticker
(red & gold)
found on dolls.

139. Nippon
(notice reversal of first N)
found incised on items

NIPPON
D13495

140. Nippon D13495
found in green

NIPPON
E

141. Nippon E
found incised on dolls

O
NIPPON

142. Nippon O
found incised on dolls

5
NIPPON

143. Nippon 5
found incised on dolls

97
NIPPON

144. Nippon 97
found incised on dolls

98
NIPPON

145. Nippon 98
found incised on dolls

99
NIPPON

146. Nippon 99
found incised on dolls

101
NIPPON

147. Nippon 101
found incised on dolls

102
NIPPON

148. Nippon 102
found incised on dolls

105 NIPPON

149. Nippon 105
found incised on dolls

123 NIPPON

150. Nippon 123
found incised on dolls

151. Nippon 144
with symbol found incised on dolls

152. RE Nippon

153. RE
made in Nippon
found incised on dolls

154. RE Nippon A9
found incised on dolls

155. RE Nippon B8
found incised on dolls

156. RE Nippon
O 2
found incised on dolls

157. Royal Hinode Nippon
found in blue

158. Sonny sticker
(gold, red, white & blue)
found on dolls

159. Maruta Royal Blue Nippon

160. Hand Painted
Coronation Ware
Nippon

161. ATA Imperial Nippon

162. Baby Doll, M.W. & Co. Nippon
Sticker found on doll

163. BE, 4 Nippon

164. Cherry blossom Nippon
Similar to No. 4

165. Cherry blossom (double) Nippon

166. C O L Nippon

167. C.O.N. Hand Painted Nippon

168. FY Nippon 405

169. FY Nippon 505

170. FY Nippon 601

171. FY Nippon 602

172. FY Nippon 1602

173. FY Nippon 603 No. 76018

174. Happifat Nippon
Sticker found on dolls

175. H in circle Nippon

176. Horsman Nippon, B9

177. James Studio China logo used in conjunction with Crown Nippon mark

178. JPL Hand Painted Nippon

KENILWORTH
STVDIOS

No. 16034
HandPainted
NIPPON

179.   Kenilworth Studios Nippon

180.   Komaru symbol, Hand Painted Nippon

181.   Komaru symbol, Hand Painted Nippon
No. 16034
Note: Japanese characters are ficticious

M
NIPPON
10

182.   M Nippon 10

183.   M Nippon, F24

184.   Manikin Nippon
Sticker found on dolls

NIPPON
3

A3
NIPPON

185.   Meiyo China Y in circle Nippon

186.   Nippon 3

187.   Nippon A3

188. Nippon 144

189. Nippon with symbol

190. Nippon with symbol

191. Nippon with symbol

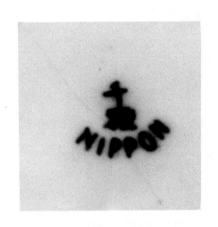

192. Nippon with symbol

193. Nippon with symbol

194. Nippon with symbol

195. Nippon with symbol

196. Nippon with symbol
Note: Japanese characters are ficticious

197. Nippon with symbol

198. Nippon with symbol, H in diamond, 14 B, P. 4.

199. Noritake M in wreath Nippon
M = Morimura Bros.
Found in green, blue and magenta
Derby indicates pattern

200. Noritake M in wreath Nippon
M = Morimura Bros.
Sahara indicates pattern

201. Noritake M in wreath Nippon
M = Morimura Bros.
The Kiva indicates pattern

202. Noritake M in wreath Nippon
M = Morimura Bros.
The Metz indicates pattern

203. Noritake M in wreath Nippon
M = Morimura Bros.

204. Noritake M in wreath Hand Painted
Nippon
M = Morimura Bros.
Marguerite indicates pattern

205. Noritake M in wreath Hand Painted Nippon
M = Morimura Bros.
Sedan indicates pattern

206. Noritake M in wreath Hand Painted Nippon
M = Morimura Bros.
The Vitry indicates pattern

207. NPMC Nippon Hand Painted

208. RC Noritake Nippon
Waverly indicates pattern

209. RE Nippon 1120

210. RE Nippon 04

211. RE Nippon B 9

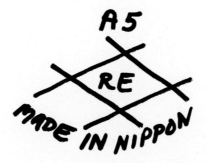

212. RE Made in Nippon A 4

213. RE Made in Nippon A 5

214. RE Made in Nippon B 9

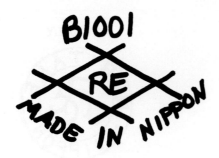

215.   RE Made in Nippon B1001

216.   Royal Kuyu Nippon

217.   S in circle Nippon

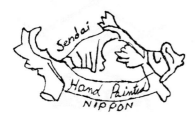

218.   Sendai Hand Painted Nippon

219.   Stouffer Hand Painted Nippon

220.   Tanega Hand Painted Nippon

221.   Torii Nippon
       Similar to No. 113

Plate 1211 - Two-piece bolted cobalt and scenic urn, 18″ tall, blue mark #52

Plate 1212 - Bolted two-piece cobalt and floral urn, 9¼″ tall, blue mark #52

Plate 1213 - Cobalt two-piece urn, 15¾″ tall, green mark #47

Plate 1214 - Bolted cobalt and scenic urn, 19″ tall, blue mark #52

Plate 1215 - Cobalt and floral vase, 7¾" tall, blue mark #52

Plate 1216 - Cobalt and floral vase, 7" tall, green mark #47

Plate 1217 - Cobalt and floral vase, 7¼" tall, blue mark #52

Plate 1218 - Cobalt and floral vase, 4½" tall, blue mark #52

Plate 1219 - Cobalt and floral vase, 15" tall, unmarked

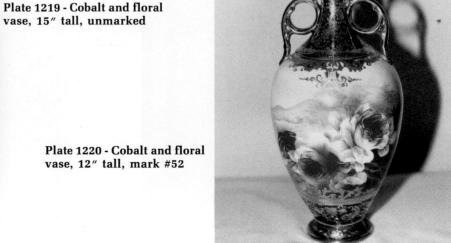

Plate 1220 - Cobalt and floral vase, 12" tall, mark #52

Plate 1221 - Pair of cobalt and scenic vases, each 8½″ tall, blue mark #52

Plate 1222 - Cobalt and scenic vase, 12½″ tall, blue mark #52

Plate 1223 - Cobalt and scenic vase, 9″ tall, green mark #52

Plate 1224 - Cobalt and scenic vase, 10″ tall, blue mark #52

Plate 1225 - Pair of cobalt and scenic vases, 5½″ tall, blue mark #52

Plate 1226 - Cobalt and scenic vase, 8½" tall, blue mark #52

Plate 1227 - Cobalt and scenic vase, 8" tall, blue mark #52

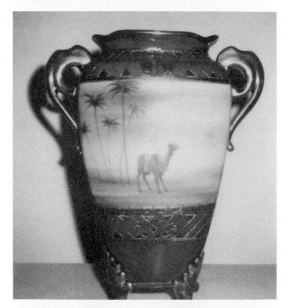

Plate 1229 - Cobalt and scenic vase, 10" tall, mark #47

Plate 1228 - Pair of cobalt and scenic vases, 8" tall, green mark #47

Plate 1230 - Cobalt and scenic vase, 8½" tall, mark #47

Plate 1231a - Pair of cobalt and scenic vases, 12″ tall, mark #42

Plate 1231b - Reverse side of cobalt vases shown in plate 1231a

Plate 1232 - Cobalt and scenic vase, 4½″ tall, mark #47

Plate 1233 - Cobalt and gold vase, 6″ tall, blue mark #52

Plate 1234 - Cobalt and scenic vase, 4¾″ tall, blue mark #52

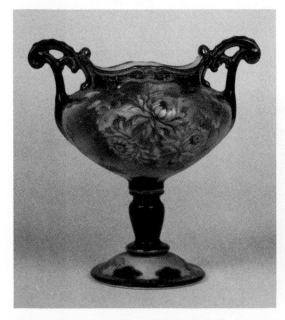

Plate 1235 - Cobalt and floral bolted vase, magenta mark #52

Plate 1236 - Pair of vases, 8¾″ tall, blue mark #84

Plate 1237 - Cobalt and scenic vase, 3½″ tall, miniature in size, could possibly have been a salesman's sample, blue mark #52

Plate 1238 - Cobalt and scenic ewer, 5¾″ tall, blue mark #52

Plate 1239 - Cobalt and scenic vase, 10″ tall, blue mark #52

Plate 1240 - Cobalt and scenic vase, 10¾″ tall, blue mark #52

Plate 1241 - Cobalt and scenic vase, 9″ tall, mark #47

Plate 1242 - Cobalt and gold vase, 4½″ tall, blue mark #52

Plate 1243 - Pair of cobalt and gold vases, each is 6¾″ tall, blue mark #52

Plate 1244 - Cobalt and scenic vase, 14″ tall, blue mark #52

Plate 1245 - Pair of cobalt and scenic vases, 10″ tall, blue mark #52

Plate 1246 - Cobalt and scenic vase, 9″ tall, mark #47

Plate 1247 - Cobalt and scenic vase, 6½″ tall, blue mark #52

Plate 1248 - Cobalt and floral tankard, 16″ tall, unmarked

Plate 1249 - Scenic vase, 6¾″ tall, green mark #47

Plate 1250 - Cobalt and scenic chocolate set (comes with six cups and saucers), creamer and sugar bowl, pot is 11″ tall, all pieces have blue mark #52

Plate 1251 - Cobalt and floral chocolate set, pot is 10½″ tall, mark #52

Plate 1252 - Cobalt and floral chocolate pot, 10¼″ tall, blue mark #52

Plate 1253 - Cobalt chocolate set, pot is 10½″ tall, blue mark #52

Plate 1254 - Cobalt and floral chocolate set, pot is 11″ tall, blue mark #52

Plate 1255 - Cobalt and scenic chocolate pot, 12″ tall, mark #52

Plate 1256 - Cobalt and floral pitcher, 7¾″ tall, unmarked

Plate 1257 - Cobalt and gold tea set, pot is 6¼″ tall, mark #73, set comes with 4 cups & saucers

107

Plate 1259 - Cobalt and floral cake plate, 10½" across, green mark #52

Plate 1258 - Cobalt and floral serving tray, 12" wide, green mark #52

Plate 1261 - Cobalt and floral pancake server, blue mark #52

Plate 1260 - Cobalt and floral bowl, 7¾" wide, green mark #52

Plate 1262 - Cobalt and floral cake server, 10¾" wide, green mark #52

Plate 1263 - Cobalt and floral plate, 10" in diameter, blue mark #52

Plate 1264 - Cobalt and floral two-piece punch or fruit bowl, 10″ across, green mark #52

Plate 1265 - Cobalt and floral ferner, 8″ wide, blue mark #52

Plate 1266 - Cobalt and floral compote, 4″ tall, green mark #52

Plate 1267 - Cobalt and floral bowl, 8¼″ wide, blue mark #52

Plate 1268 - Cobalt and floral celery dish, 13¼″ long, blue mark #52

Plate 1269 - Cobalt and floral sugar shaker, 4¼″ tall, blue mark #52

Plate 1270 - Cobalt and scenic plate, 10″ in diameter, blue mark #52

Plate 1271 - Cobalt and scenic plate, 10″ wide, green mark #47

Plate 1272 - Cobalt and scenic plate, 6½″ wide, green mark #47

Plate 1273 - Cobalt and scenic plate, 7½″ wide, artist signed "R. Otake", mark #10

Plate 1274 - Cobalt and floral plate, 10″ wide, blue mark #52

Plate 1275 - Cobalt and gold bouillon cups, 5″ tall, green mark #47

Plate 1276 - Cobalt and floral plate, 10″ wide, blue mark #52

Plate 1277 - Cobalt and scenic two-piece punch or fruit bowl, 12″ wide, 6¾″ tall, mark #47

Plate 1278 - Cobalt and gold bowl, 7½″ wide, blue mark #52

Plate 1279 - Cobalt and scenic compote, 2¼″ tall, 5″ wide, green mark #52

Plate 1280 - Cobalt and floral calling card tray, 7½″ long, green mark #47

Plate 1281 - Cobalt and gold dresser set, tray is 11¼″ long, blue mark #47

Plate 1282 - Cobalt and floral tea strainer, 6″ long, blue mark #52

Plate 1283 - Cobalt and floral tea strainer, 6¼″ long, green mark #47

Plate 1284 - Cobalt and scenic ferner, 8¼″ wide, green mark #47

Plate 1285 - Tapestry ewer, 11″ tall, blue mark #52

Plate 1286 - Tapestry vase, 7¼″ tall, blue mark #52; tapestry ewer, 7″ tall, blue mark #52

Plate 1287 - Tapestry vase, 8¼″ tall, blue mark #52

Plate 1288 - Tapestry vase, 6¼″ tall, blue mark #52

Plate 1289 - Tapestry vase, 8¼″ tall, blue mark #52

Plate 1290 - Tapestry vase, 8″ tall, blue mark #52

Plate 1291 - Tapestry vase, 8¼″ tall, green mark #52

Plate 1292 - Tapestry and moriage vases, 13″ tall, mark #91

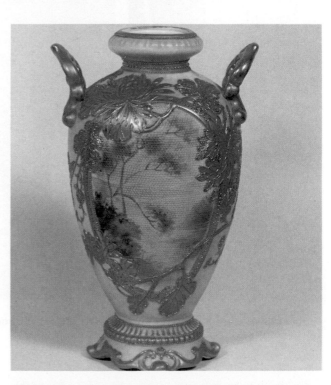

Plate 1293 - Tapestry vase, 7″ tall, mark #4

Plate 1294 - Tapestry vase, 6¼″ tall, blue mark #52

Plate 1295 - Wedgwood vase, 6¾″ tall, green mark #47

Plate 1296 - Wedgwood vase, 7¾″ tall, green mark #47

Plate 1297 - Wedgwood vase, 8½″ tall, black mark #103

Plate 1298 - Wedgwood vase, 10½″ tall, green mark #47

Plate 1299 - Wedgwood vase, 5″ tall, green mark #47

Plate 1300 - Wedgwood vase, 6¾″ tall, green mark #47

Plate 1301 - Wedgwood ferner 4″ tall, green mark #47.

Plate 1302 - Wedgwood tray, 10″ wide, green mark #47.

Plate 1303 - Wedgwood tea set, teapot is 4¾″ tall, green mark #47.

Plate 1304 - Wedgwood humidor with match holder finial, 6½″ tall, green mark #47.

Plate 1305 - Wedgwood tea set, includes six cups and saucers, teapot is 6½″ tall, green mark #47.

Plate 1306 - Wedgwood vase, 7″ tall, green mark #47

Plate 1307 - Wedgwood condensed milk container, 5½″ tall, green mark #47

Plate 1308 - Wedgwood combination matchbox holder and ashtray, 3½″ tall, green mark #47

Plate 1309 - Wedgwood nappy, 6″ across, green mark #47

Plate 1310 - Wedgwood bowl, 9¾″ wide, green mark #47

Plate 1311 - Wedgwood relish dish, 7½″ long, green mark #47

116

Plate 1312 - Wedgwood three-compartment dish, 7″ wide, green mark #47

Plate 1313 - Wedgwood compote, 9½″ wide, 2¾″ tall, green mark #47

Plate 1314 - Wedgwood bowl, 9½″ long, green mark #47

Plate 1315 - Wedgwood vase, 8″ tall, green mark #47

Plate 1316 - Wedgwood bowl, 12″ long, green mark #47

Plate 1317 - Wedgwood tray, 10½″ long, green mark #47

Plate 1318 - Wedgwood jam jar with underplate and ladle, 5½″ tall, green mark #47

Plate 1319 - Wedgwood covered box, 3½″ tall, green mark #47

Plate 1320 - Wedgwood compote, 8½″ wide, green mark #47

Plate 1321 - Wedgwood bowl, 7″ wide, green mark #47

Plate 1322 - Wedgwood compote, 4¾″ tall, 8½″ wide, green mark #47

Plate 1323 - Wedgwood and floral compote supported by three griffins, 7¾″ wide, green mark #47

Plate 1325 - Wedgwood stick vase, 9″ tall, unmarked Wedgwood ashtray, 7″ wide, blue mark #52

Plate 1324 - Wedgwood syrup with underplate, 3½″ tall, green mark #47

Plate 1326 - Wedgwood style vase, 9″ tall, green mark #47

Plate 1327 - Wedgwood style vase, 9½″ tall, green mark #47

Plate 1328 - Wedgwood style vases, 7¼" tall, green mark #47

Plate 1329 - Wedgwood style tea set, teapot is 6½" tall, mark #47

Plate 1330 - Wedgwood scenic vase, 9½″ tall, green mark #47

Plate 1331 - Wedgwood scenic vase, 7″ tall, mark #47

Plate 1332 - Wedgwood and scenic ferner, 5½″ tall, mark #47

Plate 1333 - Reverse Wedgwood ashtray, blue on cream, 3″ tall, green mark #47

Plate 1334 - Wedgwood style scenic vase, 9″ tall, green mark #47

Plate 1335a - Reverse Wedgwood vase, blue on cream, base is made up of three griffins, 8¾″ tall, green mark #47

Plate 1335b - Side view of Plate 1335a

Plate 1336 - Wedgwood candlesticks in lavender color, 7½″ tall, green mark #47

Plate 1337 - Wedgwood rose bowl in lavender color, 5¾″ tall, green mark #47

Plate 1338 - Wedgwood smoke set in lavender color, tray is 10¼" long, green mark #47

Plate 1339 - Wedgwood compote in lavender color, 5¼" tall, green mark #47

Plate 1340 - Wedgwood vase with taupe Wedgwood trim, 10¾" tall, green mark #47

Plate 1342a - Wedgwood tea set in green color, green mark #47, set comes with 4 cups & saucers

Plate 1341 Wedgwood vase with taupe Wedgwood trim, 11" tall, green mark #47

Plate 1342b - Close-up of tea cup and saucer in Plate 1342a

Plate 1343 - Portrait wall plaque, 8¾″ in diameter, blue mark #52

Plate 1344a - Portrait wall plaque, 10″ in diameter, blue mark #52

Plate 1344b - Close-up of workmanship displayed in Plate 1344a

Plate 1345 - Portrait wall plaque, 9½″ in diameter, blue mark #52

Plate 1346 - Portrait wall plaque, 12½″ in diameter, blue mark #52

Plate 1347 - Cobalt portrait two-piece bolted urn, 16″ tall, green mark #52

Plate 1348 - Portrait lamp, vase base is 9½″ tall, blue mark #52

Plate 1349 - Portrait vase, 6″ tall, mark #52

Plate 1350 - Cobalt portrait vase, 7½″ tall, green mark #52

Plate 1351 - Portrait basket vase, 7½″ tall, blue mark #52

Plate 1352 - Portrait lamp, 35″ from top of fixture to bottom, green mark #52

Plate 1353 - Portrait vase, 16″ tall, green mark #52

Plate 1354 - Portrait vase, 12½″ tall, green mark #52

Plate 1355 - Portrait vase, 12½″ tall, green mark #52

Plate 1356 - Portait covered urn, 10″ tall, blue mark #52

Plate 1357 - Portrait vase, 5¾″ tall, blue mark #52

Plate 1358 - Portrait vase, 7¼″ tall, green mark #52

Plate 1359 - Portrait plate, 10″ in diameter, green mark #52

Plate 1360 - Portrait vase, 9″ tall, blue mark #52

Plate 1361 - Portrait wall plaque, 10″ in diameter, blue mark #52

Plate 1362 - Portrait wall plaque, 10″ in diameter, blue mark #52

Plate 1363 - Portrait vase, 5½" tall, blue mark #52

Plate 1364 - Portrait vase, 7¼" tall, blue mark #52

Plate 1365 - Two piece bolted portrait urn, 12" tall, blue mark #52

Plate 1366 - Portrait vase, 11¼" tall, unmarked

128

Plate 1367 - Portrait ewer, 6¾" tall, blue mark #52

Plate 1368 - Portrait powder box, blue mark #52

Plate 1369 - Portrait vase, 8¾" tall, unmarked

Plate 1370 - Portrait hatpin holder, 5" tall, blue mark #52

Plate 1371 - Portrait bouillon cup and cover, 4" tall, blue mark #52

Plate 1372 - Portrait ewer, 6¾" tall, blue mark #52

Plate 1373 - Portrait vase, 10½" tall, blue mark #52

Plate 1374 - Portrait vase, 8¾" tall, green mark #47

Plate 1376 - Portrait vase, 7¼" tall, blue mark #52

Plate 1375 - Portrait vase, 6½" tall, blue mark #52

Plate 1377 - Portrait covered urn, 8" tall, blue mark #52

Plate 1441 - Moriage vase, 8¾" tall, mark #52

Plate 1442 - Moriage cake set, master serving dish is 10¾" in diameter, small ones are 6", mark #47, set comes with 6 small plates

Plate 1443 - Moriage ewer, 10" tall, blue mark #52

Plate 1444 - Moriage vase, 12½" tall, mark #91

Plate 1445 - Moriage ewer, 10" tall, blue mark #52

Plate 1446 - Moriage mug, 5" tall, blue mark #52

Plate 1447 - Moriage covered urn, 11" tall, mark #90

143

Plate 1449 - Gouda style candlestick, 7½″ tall, green mark #47; Gouda style cake plate, 7″ wide, green mark #47

Plate 1448 - Gouda style basket vase, 7″ tall, green mark #47

Plate 1450 - Gouda style candlesticks, 8″ tall, green mark #47; Gouda style tray, 8″ wide, green mark #47

Plate 1451 - Gouda style basket vase, 7″ tall, green mark #47

Plate 1452 - "Sponge" tapestry vase, 9½" tall, blue mark #52

Plate 1453 - Vase, pattern stamped, 5½" tall, green mark #47

Plate 1454 - Vase, pattern stamped, 8" tall, green mark #47

Plate 1455 - Vase, pattern stamped, 5½" tall, green mark #47

145

Plate 1456 - Demitasse set, silver overlay, pot is 6″ tall, mark #82

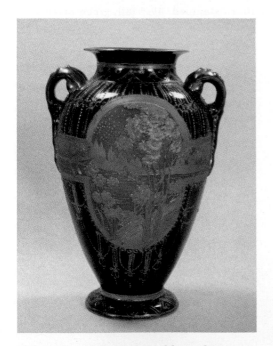

Plate 1457 - Cobalt and gold overlay vase, 8½″ tall, blue mark #52

Plate 1458 - Beaded nappy, 6¼″ wide, blue mark #110

Plate 1459 - Beaded chocolate set, pot is 11″ tall, all pieces unmarked

Plate 1460 - Plate, 9″ in diameter, Souvenir of Washington, D.C., blue mark #52

Plate 1461 - Vase, 7½″ tall, Souvenir of Washington, D.C., blue mark #52

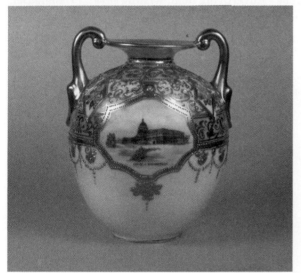

Plate 1462 - Vase, 5″ tall, Souvenir of Washington, D.C., mark #52

Plate 1463 - Candy dish, Souvenir of Washington, D.C., 6½″ long, blue mark #37

Plate 1464 - Cup and saucer, Souvenir of "Business Section From Waterfront, Seattle, Washington", mark #100

Plate 1465a - Trinket box, 3¼″ in diameter, green mark #47

Plate 1466a - Advertising item, writing says "Triangle Dentifrice", covered box is 3¾″ wide, mark #110

Plate 1465b - Inside of lid of trinket box in Plate 1465a; "The Wonder Millinery, Corner Alder and Sixth Streets, Portland, Oregon"

Plate 1466b - Side view of trinket box in Plate 1466a

Plate 1467 - Rolling pin, porcelain body is 9¾″ long, mark #84

All Items Molded In Relief

Plate 1468 - Wall plaque, 14″ long, green mark #47

Plate 1469 - Wall plaque, similar to Plate 123, 10½″ wide, green mark #47

Plate 1470 - Wall plaque, 10½″ wide, green mark #47

Plate 1471 - Hanging wall plaque, 10½″ wide, similar to Plate 118 except coloring is different, green mark #47

Plate 1472 - Wall plaque, 12″ wide, similar to Plate 1473, green mark #47

Plate 1473 - Wall plaque, 12″ wide, similar to plate in Plate 1472, green mark #47

All Items Molded In Relief

Plate 1474 - Wall plaque, 18½″ long, green mark #47

Plate 1475 - Wall plaque, 10½″ in diameter, green mark #47

Plate 1476 - Wall plaque, 18½″ long, green mark #47

Plate 1477 - Wall plaque, 15″ wide, similar to Plate 121, only larger, green mark #47

Plate 1478 - Wall plaque, 18½″ long, green mark #47

All Items Molded In Relief

Plate 1479 - Wall plaque, 10½″ wide, similar to Plate 117, green mark #47

Plate 1480 - Wall plaque, 10½″ wide, green mark #47

Plate 1481 - Wall plaque, 15″ wide, similar to Plate 122 only larger, green mark #47

Plate 1482 - Wall plaque, 10½″ wide, also referred to as a charger, similar to Plate 121, green mark #47

Plate 1483 - Humidor, 7″ tall, green mark #47

Plate 1484 - Ashtray, 5¾″ in diameter, green mark #47

All Items Molded In Relief

Plate 1485 - Wall plaque, 10½″ wide, green mark #47

Plate 1486 - Wall plaque, 10½″ in diameter, green mark #47

Plate 1487 - Humidor, 7½″ tall, green mark #47

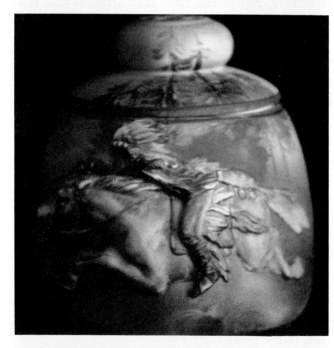

Plate 1488 - Humidor, 6½″ tall, similar to Plate 129, green mark #47

Plate 1489 - Ashtray, 2½″ high, green mark #47

Plate 1490 - Ashtray, 2½″ high, green mark #47

All Items Molded In Relief

Plate 1491a - Humidor, 7¼″ tall, green mark #47

Plate 1491b - Another view of humidor shown in Plate 1491a

Plate 1492 - Humidor, 7½″ wide, green mark #47

Plate 1493 - Humidor, 7″ tall, similar to Plate 109, green mark #47

All Items Molded In Relief

Plate 1494 - Humidor, 7″ tall, green mark #47

Plate 1495 - Humidor, 7″ tall, green mark #47

Plate 1496 - Humidor, 6½″ long, green mark #47

Plate 1497 - Humidor, 8″ tall, green mark #47

Plate 1498 - Humidor, 6¾″ tall, green mark #47

Plate 1499 - Humidor, 6½″ tall, green mark #47

All Items Molded In Relief

Plate 1500 - Humidor, 7″ tall, green mark #47

Plate 1501 - Ashtray, 6¼″ in diameter, green mark #47

Plate 1502 - Humidor, 6½″ tall, green mark #47

Plate 1503 - Inkwell, 4″ tall, green mark #47

Plate 1504 - Covered box, 3″ tall, 5½″ long, green mark #47

Plate 1505 - Bowl, 9″ wide, mark #47

All Items Molded In Relief

Plate 1506a - Ferner, 5″ in width, 4½″ tall, green mark #47

Plate 1506b - Another view of ferner in Plate 1506a

Plate 1507 - Basket dish, 7½″ wide, green mark #47

Plate 1508 - Ferner, 8¼″ long, 5½″ tall, same mold as Plate 1509, green mark #47

Plate 1509 - Ferner, 8¼″ long, 5½″ tall, same mold as Plate 1508, green mark #47

All Items Molded In Relief

Plate 1510a - Tankard set, tankard is 11½″ tall, mugs are 4¾″ tall, green mark #47

Plate 1510b - Close-up of tankard shown in Plate 1510a

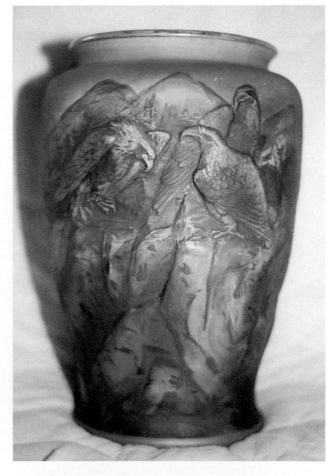

Plate 1511 - Vase, 10″ tall, green mark #47

All Items Molded In Relief

Plate 1512a - Vase, 9¼″ tall, green mark #47

Plate 1512b - Close-up of faces on vase in Plate 1512a

Plate 1513 - Vase, 12½″ tall, same as Plate 560, only shown in color, green mark #47

Plate 1514 - Vase, 10″ tall, similar to Plate 107, different coloring, green mark #47

All Items Molded In Relief

Plate 1515 - Vase, 5½" tall, green mark #47; vase, 5¾" tall, green mark #47

Plate 1517 - Vase, 10½" tall, similar to Plate 1516, green mark #47

Plate 1516 - Vase, 10½" tall, similar to Plate 1517, color variation, green mark #47

All Items Molded In Relief

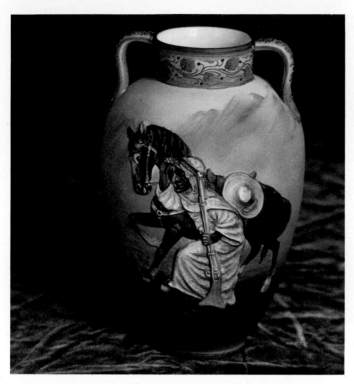

Plate 1518 - Vase, 10″ tall, green mark #47

Plate 1519 - Vase 9¾″ tall, same as Plate 559, only shown in color, green mark #47

Plate 1520 - Vase, 13½″ tall, green mark #47

Plate 1521 - Vase, 8″ tall, mark #47

All Items Molded In Relief

Plate 1522 - Vase, 8″ tall, blue mark #47

Plate 1523 - Vase, 10″ tall, green mark #47

Plate 1524 - Vase, 8¼″ tall, handle is full figure of a lizard, blue mark #52

Plate 1525 - Vase, 6″ tall, blue mark #52

Plate 1526 - Vase 10½″ tall, has glossy finish, mark #4

Plate 1527 - Vase, 8¾″ tall, green mark #47

All Items Molded In Relief

Plate 1528 - Two-handled bowl, 7½" long, green mark #47

Plate 1529a - Two-handled bowl, 8½" long, green mark #47

Plate 1530 - Nut bowl, molded in shape of a nut, 6½" long, mark #47

Plate 1529b - Close-up of Plate 1529a, showing relief work in detail

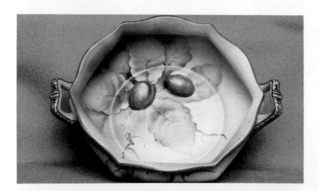

Plate 1531 - Two-handled bowl, 8½" in diameter, green mark #47

Plate 1532 - Fruit bowl, 7½" wide, green mark #47

Plate 1533 - Nut bowl, molded in shape of nut, 6½" long, green mark #47

Plate 1534 - Novelty napkin holder, 4″ tall, green mark #47

Plate 1535 - Ashtray with figural owls perched on side, 4″ tall, 7″ across, green mark #47

Plate 1536 - Figural ashtray, 6½″ long, green mark #47

Plate 1537 - Ferner with figural owls perched on side, 5″ long, green mark #47

Plate 1538a - Novelty type candy dish, 6″ wide, green mark #47

Plate 1538b - Another view of Plate 1538a

Plate 1539 - Sardine set, handle is a figural sardine, 6¼″ long, green mark #47

Plate 1540 - Figural flower arranger, 5½″ long, green mark #47

Plate 1541 - Ashtray, 6″ long, base is molded in relief with five faces. Front face has two ears, second and third faces have one horn, fourth and fifth faces have two horns, green mark #47

Plate 1542 - Novelty type vase, base is composed of three molded griffins, vase is 8¾″ tall, green mark #47

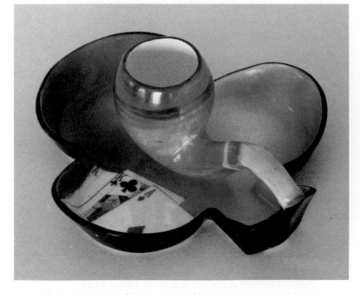

Plate 1543 - Ashtray, 5¼″ long,, green mark #47

Plate 1544 - Novelty type ashtray, see Plate 587 and Plate 1547 for others, blue mark #84

Plate 1545a - Two-piece novelty piano trinket box, 5″ in length, 2½″ tall, green mark #47

Plate 1545b - Same as Plate 1545a with cover in place.

Plate 1546 - Dogs of Foo are squatty figures with tails sticking primly up over their backs. They came from Korea and are believed to have been brought into Japan along with the teachings of Buddha. When these dogs first arrived, they were thought of as lions but now they have become dogs and are put at the entrance to temples to guard against evil influences, although it really is hard to tell from their expression whether the dogs are laughing or angry. Dogs of Foo, 9″ tall, red mark #55.

Plate 1547 - Novelty type ashtray, see Plate 587 and Plate 1544 for others, blue mark #84

Plate 1548 - Dutch shoes, each 3″ long, green mark #47

Plate 1549 - Hanging plaque, 10¼″ wide, 8″ long, green mark #47

Plate 1550 - Hanging plaque, 10¼″ long, 8″ wide, green mark #47

Plate 1551 - Hanging plaque, 10¼ wide, 8″ long, green mark #47

Plate 1552 - Hanging plaque, 10¼″ wide, green mark #47

Plate 1553 - Hanging plaque, 10¼″ wide, 8″ long, green mark #47

Plate 1554 - Hanging plaque, 12″ in diameter, green mark #47

Plate 1555 - Hanging plaque, 12″ in diameter, green mark #47

Plate 1556 - Hanging plaque, 12″ in diameter, green mark #47

Plate 1557 - Hanging plaque, 12″ in diameter, green mark #47

Plate 1558 - Hanging plaque, 12″ in diameter, green mark #47

Plate 1559 - Hanging plaque, 12″ in diameter, green mark #47

Plate 1560 - Hanging plaque, 12″ in diameter, green mark #47

Plate 1561 - Hanging plaque, 12″ in diameter, green mark #47

Plate 1562 - Hanging plaque, 10¼″ in diameter, green mark #47

Plate 1563 - Hanging plaque, 10″ wide, green mark #47

Plate 1564 - Hanging plaque, 13½″ in diameter, blue mark #52

Plate 1565 - Hanging plaque, 10″ in diameter, green mark #47

Plate 1566 - Hanging plaque, 8″ in diameter, green mark #47

Plate 1567 - Hanging, plaque, 12½″ in diameter, green mark #47

Plate 1568 - Hanging plaque, 10¼″ in diameter, green mark #47

Plate 1569 - Hanging plaque, 10″ in diameter, blue mark #52

Plate 1570 - Hanging plaque, 9″ in diameter, green mark #47

Plate 1571 - Hanging plaque, 10″ in diameter, green mark #47

Plate 1572 - Hanging plaque, 8″ in diameter, green mark #47

Plate 1573 - Hanging plaque, 10″ in diameter, blue mark #47

Plate 1574 - Hanging plaque, 9″ in diameter, green mark #47

Plate 1575 - Hanging plaque, 10″ in diameter, gold overlay, blue mark #52

Plate 1576 - Hanging plaque, 10″ in diameter, green mark #47

Plate 1577 - Hanging plaque, 8½″ in diameter, blue mark #47

Plate 1578 - Hanging plaque, 10″ in diameter, green mark #47

Plate 1579 - Hanging plaque, 10″ in diameter, green mark #47

Plate 1580 - Hanging plaque, 8″ in diameter, green mark #47

Plate 1581 - Hanging plaque, 8″ in diameter, green mark #47

Plate 1582 - Hanging plaque, 7¾″ in diameter, green mark #47

Plate 1583 - Hanging plaque, 10″ in diameter, green mark #47

Plate 1584 - Hanging plaque, 10″ in diameter, blue mark #52

Plate 1585 - Hanging plaque, 12¼″ in diameter, green mark #47

Plate 1586 - Hanging plaque, 7¾″ in diameter, green mark #47

Plate 1587 - Hanging plaque, 9″ in diameter, green mark #47

Plate 1588 - Hanging plaque, 11″ in diameter, green mark #47

Plate 1589 - Hanging plaque, 10″ in diameter, green mark #47

Plate 1590 - Hanging plaque, 9″ in diameter, green mark #47

Plate 1591 - Hanging plaque, 9″ in diameter, blue mark #47

Plate 1592 - Hanging plaque, 7¾″ in diameter, green mark #47

Plate 1593 - Hanging plaque, 10″ in diameter, blue mark #47

Plate 1594 - Hanging plaque, 10¾″ in diameter, mark #47

Plate 1595 - Hanging plaque, 10″ in diameter, green mark #47

Plate 1596 - Hanging plaque, 9″ in diameter, green mark #47

Plate 1597 - Hanging plaque, 10″ in diameter, green mark #47

Plate 1598 - Hanging plaque, 7¾″ in diameter, blue mark #47

Plate 1599 - Hanging plaque, 9″ in diameter, green mark #47

Plate 1600 - Hanging plaque, 7¾″ in diameter, green mark #47

Plate 1601 - Hanging plaque, 10″ in diameter, green mark #47

Plate 1602 - Hanging plaque, 9″ in diameter, green mark #47

Plate 1603 - Hanging plaque, 8¾″ in diameter, green mark #47

Plate 1604 - Hanging plaque, 11″ in diameter, blue mark #52

Plate 1605 - Hanging plaque, 9″ in diameter, green mark #47

Plate 1606 - Hanging plaque, 10″ in diameter, green mark #47

Plate 1607 - Hanging plaque, 9½″ in diameter, blue mark #52

175

Plate 1608 - Hanging plaque, 10″ in diameter, green mark #47

Plate 1609 - Hanging plaque, 9″ in diameter, green mark #47

Plate 1610 - Hanging plaque, 10″ in diameter, green mark #47

Plate 1611 - Hanging plaque, 10″ in diameter, green mark #47

Plate 1612 - Hanging plaque, 9″ in diameter, green mark #47

Plate 1613 - Hanging plaque, 10″ in diameter, green mark #27

Plate 1614 - Hanging plaque, 10″ in diameter, green mark #47

Plate 1615 - Hanging plaque, 10″ in diameter, green mark #47

Plate 1616 - Hanging plaque, 9″ in diameter, green mark #47

Plate 1617 - Hanging plaque, 10″ in diameter, green mark #47

Plate 1618 - Hanging plaque, 7¾″ in diameter, green mark #47

Plate 1619 - Hanging plaque, 10″ in diameter, green mark #47

177

Plate 1620 - Hanging plaque, 9½″ in diameter, blue mark #52

Plate 1621 - Hanging plaque, 10″ in diameter, green mark #47

Plate 1622 - Hanging plaque, 11″ in diameter, green mark #47

Plate 1623 - Hanging plaque, 10″ in diameter, green mark #47

Plate 1624 - Hanging plaque, 10″ in diameter, green mark #47

Plate 1625 - Hanging plaque, 10″ in diameter, green mark #47

Plate 1626 - Hanging plaque, 7¾" in diameter, green mark #47

Plate 1627 - Hanging plaque, 10" in diameter, gold overlay trim, blue mark #52

Plate 1628 - Hanging plaque, 10" in diameter, blue mark #52

Plate 1629 - Hanging plaque, 10" in diameter, blue mark #47

Plate 1630 - Hanging plaque, 10" in diameter, green mark #47

Plate 1631 - Hanging plaque, 10" in diameter, green mark #47

Plate 1632 - Hanging plaque, 7¾″ in diameter, green mark #47

Plate 1633 - Hanging plaque, 10″ in diameter, blue mark #47

Plate 1634 - Hanging plaque, 11″ in diameter, green mark #47

Plate 1635 - Hanging plaque, 10″ in diameter, blue mark #47

Plate 1636 - Hanging plaque, 11″ in diameter, green mark #47

Plate 1637 - Hanging plaque, 8¾″ in diameter, blue mark #52

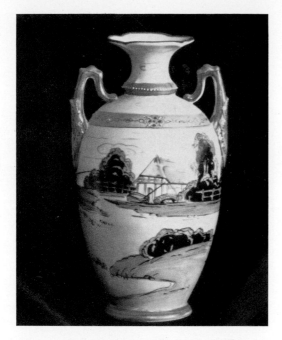

Plate 1638 - Vase, 9¾″ tall, green mark #52

Plate 1639 - Vase, 11¾″ tall, blue mark #52

Plate 1640 - Vase, 6½″ tall, mark #52

Plate 1641 - Vase, 5½″ tall, blue mark #52

Plate 1642 - Vase, 8¼″ tall, green mark #47

Plate 1643 - Vase, 7¼″ tall, green mark #47

Plate 1644 - Pair of vases, 8¾" tall, green mark #47

Plate 1645 - Vase, 5½" tall, green mark #47

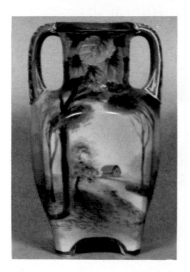

Plate 1646 - Vase, 7" tall, mark #47

Plate 1647 - Pair of vases, 9¼" tall, green mark #47

Plate 1648 - Vase, 8" tall, green mark #47; vase, 7½" tall, blue mark #52

Plate 1649 - Vase, 6½" tall, green mark #47

Plate 1650 - Pair of vases, 14″ tall, mark #47

Plate 1651 - Vase, 17½″ tall, mark #47

Plate 1652 - Vase, 10½″ tall, green mark #47

Plate 1654 - Vase, 9½″ tall, green
mark #47

Plate 1655 - Vase, 12″ tall, mark #17

Plate 1653 - Vase, 12½″ tall,
mark #47

Plate 1657 - Vase, 8½″ tall, green mark #47

Plate 1656 - Loving cup vase, 4¼″ tall, green
mark #47

Plate 1658 - Vase, 10″ tall, blue
mark #52

184

Plate 1659 - Vase, 12″ tall, mark #47

Plate 1660 - Pair of vases, 10¾″ tall, green mark #47

Plate 1661 - Vase, 14½″ tall, green mark #47

Plate 1662 - Pair of vases, 3″ tall, mark #47

Plate 1663 - Vase, 10″ tall, green mark #47

Plate 1664 - Vase, 5½″ tall, mark #103

Plate 1665 - Pair of vases, 9½″ tall; larger vase, 12½″ tall, green mark #47

Plate 1666 - Vase, 11¼" tall, gold overlay trim, blue mark #52

Plate 1667 - Vase, 5¼" tall, green mark #47

Plate 1668 - Vase, 5" tall, green mark #47

Plate 1669 - Small vase, 4½" tall, green mark #47; large vase, 12" tall, green mark #52

Plate 1670 - Vase, 9½" tall, blue mark #52

Plate 1671 - Vase, 12″ tall, green mark #47

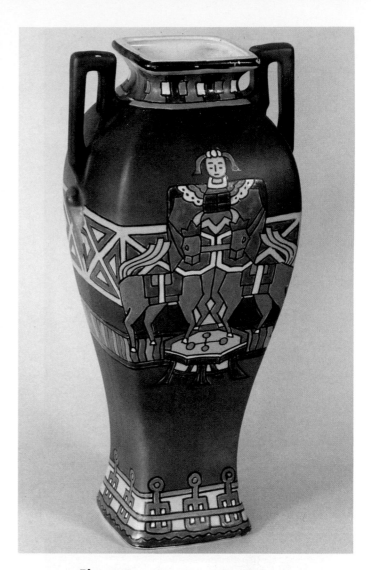

Plate 1672 - Vase, 12″ tall, mark #91

Plate 1673 - Vase, 13″ tall, green mark #47

Plate 1674 - Vase, 10″ tall, blue mark #47

Plate 1675 - Ewer vase, 7½″ tall, green mark #47

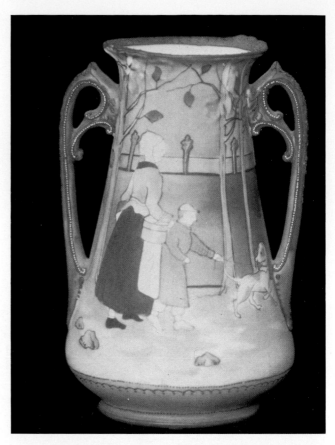

Plate 1676 - Vase, 7″ tall, blue mark #47

Plate 1677 - Vase, 10½″ tall, green mark #47

Plate 1678 - Vase, 13½″ tall, blue mark #52

Plate 1679 - Vase, 5¾″ tall, green mark #47

Plate 1680 - Vase, 11½″ tall, blue mark #47

Plate 1681 - Vase, 10″ tall, mark #47

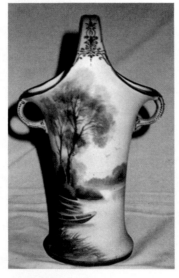

Plate 1682 - Basket vase, 11″ tall, green mark #47

Plate 1863 - Vase, 4¼″ tall, green mark #47

Plate 1684 - Vase, 10″ tall, green mark #47

Plate 1685 - Vase, 12″ tall, mark #47

Plate 1686 - Vase, 6½″ tall, green mark #47

Plate 1687 - Vase, 6¼″ tall, green mark #47

Plate 1688 - Left to right: vase, 6″ tall; vase, 5″ tall; vase, 5½″ tall; all green mark #47

Plate 1689 - Vase, 4½″ tall, green mark #47

Plate 1690 - Pair of vases, 8″ tall, green mark #47

Plate 1691 - Vase, 5″ tall, green mark #47

Plate 1692 - Vase, 12½″ tall, green mark #47

Plate 1693 - Vase, 11¼″ tall, green mark #47

Plate 1694 - Vase, 8″ tall, mark #47

Plate 1695 - Vase, 12″ tall, mark #47

Plate 1696 - Vase, 24½″ tall, green mark #47

Plate 1697 - Vase, 12½″ tall, blue mark #52

Plate 1698 - Vase, 12″ tall, red mark #110

Plate 1699 - Vase, 13½″ tall, green mark #47

Plate 1700 - Vase, 12¼″ tall, blue mark #52

Plate 1701 - Vase, 7″ tall, green mark #47

Plate 1702 - Vase, 8″ tall, blue mark #47

Plate 1703 - Vase, 10½″ tall, blue mark #47

Plate 1704 - Vase, 15″ tall, mark #52

Plate 1705 - Vase, 8¾″ tall, green mark #47

Plate 1706 - Vase, 7½″ tall, green mark #47

Plate 1707 - Vase, 7″ tall, mark #179

193

Plate 1708 - Vase, 13″ tall, mark #47

Plate 1709 - Vase, 17½″ tall, mark #47

Plate 1710 - Vase 9½″ tall, green mark #47

Plate 1711 - Vase, 6″ tall, green mark #47

Plate 1712 - Vase, 13″ tall, green mark #47

Plate 1713 - Vase, 11″ tall, green mark #47

Plate 1714 - Vase, 7½″ tall, green mark #7

Plate 1715 - Vase, 8½″ tall, mark #52

Plate 1716 - Vase, 10¼″ tall, gold overlay trim, green mark #47

Plate 1717 - Vase, 10¼″ tall, gold overlay trim, green mark #47

Plate 1719 - Vase, 11¾″ tall, green mark #47

Plate 1718 - Vase, 13½″ tall, mark #47

Plate 1721 - Vase, 14″ tall, mark #47

Plate 1720 - Vase, 10½″ tall, mark #47

Plate 1722 - Vase 5″ tall, green mark #47

Plate 1723 - Vase, 10″ tall, mark #47

Plate 1724 - Vase, 11″ tall, green mark #47

Plate 1725 - Vase, 13¼″ tall, mark #38

Plate 1726 - Vase, 9½″ tall, mark #38

Plate 1727 - Vase, 13″ tall, mark #52

Plate 1728 - Vase, 12″ tall, mark #38

Plate 1729 - Vase, 4½″ tall, green mark #47

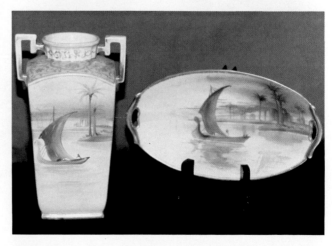

Plate 1730 - Vase, 8″ tall; celery dish, 8½″ long; both green mark #47

197

Plate 1731 - Vase, 9½″ tall, green mark #47

Plate 1732 - Vase, 7¾″ tall, green mark #47

Plate 1733 - Vase, 7½″ tall, green mark #47

Plate 1734 - Vase, 10¼″ tall, green mark #47

Plate 1735 - Vase, 6″ tall, green mark #47

Plate 1736 - Vase, 11½″ tall, blue mark #38

Plate 1737 - Vase, 14″ tall, blue mark #71

Plate 1738 - Vase, 7½″ tall, mark #47

Plate 1739 - Vase, 12¾″ tall, green mark #47

Plate 1740 - Vase, 6″ tall, green mark #47

Plate 1741 - Pair of vases, 13½″ tall, mark #47

Plate 1742 - Vase, 9″ tall, green mark #47

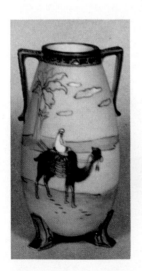

**Plate 1743 - Vase,
5½″ tall, green mark
#47**

**Plate 1744 - Inkwell, 3½″ tall; vase, 8″ tall; sugar bowl, 4½″ tall; all green
mark #47**

Plate 1745 - Vase, 11″ tall, green mark #47

Plate 1746 - Vase, 6″ tall, green mark #47

Plate 1747 - Vase, 8½″ tall, green mark #47

Plate 1748 - Vase, 9″ tall, mark #47

Plate 1749 - Vase, 7¼″ tall, blue mark #52

Plate 1750 - Vase, 5½″ tall, blue mark #52

Plate 1751 - Vase, 10″ tall, green mark #47

Plate 1752 - Vase, 18″ tall, blue mark #52

Plate 1753 - Vase, 9¼″ tall, green mark #47

Plate 1754 - Vase, 8″ tall, green mark #47

Plate 1755 - Vase, 8¾″ tall, green mark #47

Plate 1756 - Vase, 24″ tall, blue mark #52

Plate 1757 - Vase, 9¾″ tall, green mark #47

Plate 1758 - Vase, 9½″ tall, blue mark #52

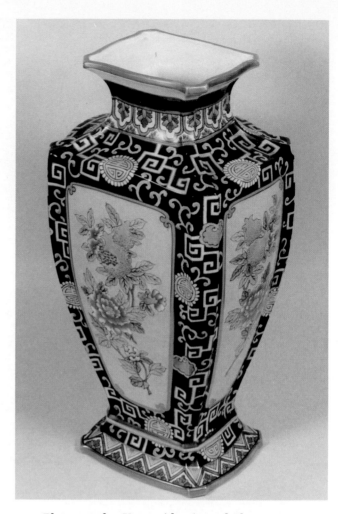

Plate 1759a - Vase, 16″ tall, green mark #47

Plate 1759b - Vase, side view of Plate 1759a

Plate 1760 - Vase, 12″ tall, green mark #47

Plate 1761 - Vase, 9¾″ tall, blue mark #52

Plate 1762 - Vase, 13½″ tall, green mark #47

Plate 1763 - Vase 14½″ tall, mark #47

Plate 1764 - Pair of vases, 5¼″ tall, green mark #47

Plate 1765 - Vase, 6″ tall, green mark #47

Plate 1766 - Vase, 15½″ tall, green mark #47

Plate 1767 - Vase, 9½″ tall, blue mark #52

Plate 1768 - Vase, 12″ tall, mark #47

Plate 1769 - Vase, 13″ tall, green mark #47

Plate 1770 - Vase, 11¼″ tall, mark #47

Plate 1771 - Vase, 8″ tall, green mark #47

Plate 1772 - Vase, 15½″ tall, mark #52

Plate 1773 - Vase, 10″ tall, mark #52

Plate 1774 - Pair of vases, 12½″ tall, blue mark #52

Plate 1775 - Two vases, each 11″ tall, both green mark #47

Plate 1776 - Vase, 9¾″ tall, green mark #47

Plate 1777 - Vase, 12″ tall, green mark
#47

Plate 1778 - Vase, 13½″ tall, mark #47

Plate 1779 - Vase, 12″ tall, blue
mark #52

Plate 1780 - Vase, 8" tall, mark #52

Plate 1781 - Vase, 14" tall, mark removed

Plate 1782 - Vase, 16½" tall, mark #47

Plate 1783 - Stick vase, 12" tall, blue mark #52

Plate 1784 - Vase, 11½" tall, mark #89

Plate 1785 - Vase, 3½" tall, 8½" long, mark #70

Plate 1786 - Vase, 11" tall, mark #47

Plate 1787 - Vase, 8½" tall, blue mark #52

Plate 1788 - Pair of vases, 6½" tall, blue mark #47

Plate 1789 - Pair of vases, 7½" tall, mark #47

Plate 1790 - Vase, 6" tall, green mark #47

Plate 1791 - Vase, 8½″ tall, with rare seahorse handles, mark #52

Plate 1792 - Vase, 9″ tall, green mark #47

Plate 1793 - Vase, 8½″ tall, has rare seahorse handles, mark #52

Plate 1794 - Vase, 3″ tall, green mark #47

Plate 1795 - Vase, 9″ tall, blue mark #52

Plate 1796 - Pair of vases, 7½″ tall, mark #52; vase in center, 5½″ tall, green mark #47

Plate 1797 - Left to right: Vase, 8″ tall, mark #52; vase, 10″ tall, mark #47; vase, 7¾″ tall, mark #52

Plate 1798 - Vase, 12″ tall, blue mark #52

Plate 1799 - Vase, 6½″ tall, green mark #47

Plate 1800 - Vase, 7½″ tall, blue mark #52

Plate 1801 - Vase, 5½″ tall, blue mark #47

Plate 1802 - Vase, 5¾″ tall, blue mark #52

Plate 1803 - Vase, 12″ tall, mark #52

212

Plate 1805 - Vase, 9″ tall, green mark #47

Plate 1804 - Vase, 18″ tall, blue mark #52

Plate 1806 - Vase, six sided, 14½″ tall, green mark #47

Plate 1807 - Vase, 9″ tall, green mark #47

Plate 1808 - Vase, 8″ tall, mark #52

Plate 1809 - Vase, 12″ tall, mark #26

Plate 1810 - Vase, 11″ tall, mark #52

Plate 1811 - Vase, 5½″ tall, blue mark #52

Plate 1812 - Vase, 5½″ tall, blue mark #52

Plate 1813 - Vase, 5½″ tall, green mark #47

Plate 1814 - Vase, 8″ tall, green mark #47

Plate 1815 - Vase, 10½″ tall, mark #52

214

Plate 1816 - Vase, 6″ tall, green mark #47

Plate 1817 - Vase, 8½ tall, green mark #47

Plate 1818 - Vase, 9½″ tall, green mark #47

Plate 1819 - Vase, 5½″ tall, green mark #47

Plate 1820 - Vase, 5″ tall, blue mark #44

Plate 1821 - Pair of vases, 7″ tall, mark #52

Plate 1822 - Vase, 9″ tall, mark #52

Plate 1823 - Vase, 13″ tall, green mark #47

Plate 1824 - Vase, 9″ tall, mark #91

Plate 1825 - Vase, 13″ tall, mark #47

Plate 1826 - Vase, 10″ tall, mark #52

Plate 1827 - Vase, 9″ tall, green mark #47

Plate 1828 - Left vase, 7″ tall, green mark #52; right vase, 7″ tall, blue mark #52

Plate 1829 - Vase, 10″ tall, mark #47

Plate 1830 - Vase, 9″ tall, green mark #47

Plate 1831 - Vase, 6½″ tall, green mark #47

Plate 1832 - Vase, 7″ tall, green mark #47

Plate 1833 - Vase, 12 tall, mark #47

Plate 1834 - Vase, 12½″ tall, mark #91

Plate 1835 - Vase, 11½″ tall, mark #52

Plate 1836 - Vase, 7″ tall, green mark #47

Plate 1837 - Vase, 12″ tall, has heavy gold trim, green mark #47

Plate 1838 - Vase, 12″ tall, mark #52

Plate 1839 - Vase, 7″ tall, green mark #47

Plate 1840 - Vase, 9½″ tall, blue mark #52

Plate 1841 - Vase, 4¼″ tall, green mark #47

Plate 1842 - Vase, 10″ tall, green mark #47

Plate 1843 - Vase, 7″ tall, mark #47

Plate 1844 - Vase, 9″ tall, green mark #47

Plate 1845 - Vase, 7″ tall, mark #52

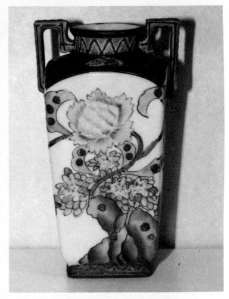

Plate 1846 - Vase, 12″ tall, green mark #52

Plate 1847 - Vase, 7″ tall, mark #47

Plate 1848 - Vase, 6½″ tall, blue mark #7

Plate 1849 - Vase, 13½″ tall, mark #52

Plate 1850 - Vase, 5¾″ tall, mark #75

Plate 1851 - Vase, 13½″ tall, green mark #47

Plate 1852 - Vase, 9½″ tall, mark #52

Plate 1853 - Vase, 7″ tall, mark #52

Plate 1854 - Vase, 8½″ tall, green mark #47

Plate 1855a - Vase, 11½″ tall, mark #91

Plate 1855b - Rear view of vase in Plate 1855a; notice how design continues around

Plate 1856 - Vase, 10″ tall, green mark #47

Plate 1857 - Vase, 6¼″ tall, green mark #47

Plate 1859 - Vase, 14½″ tall, green mark #47

Plate 1858 - Vase, 10″ tall, mark #52

Plate 1860 - Vase, 9″ tall, green mark #47

Plate 1861 - Two-piece bolted urn, 8½″ tall, green mark #47

Plate 1862 - Two-piece bolted covered urn, 19″ tall, green mark #47

Plate 1863 - Two-piece bolted urn 24½″ tall, green mark #47

Plate 1864 - Two-piece bolted urns, 27″ tall, green mark #47

Plate 1865 - Covered urn, 13″ tall, blue mark #52

Plate 1866 - Two-piece bolted urn, covered, 15¼″ tall, green mark #47

Plate 1867 - Two-piece bolted urn, 18 tall, green mark #47

Plate 1868 - Two-piece bolted urn, 18″ tall, green mark #47

Plate 1870 - Covered urn, 9½″ tall, blue mark #89

Plate 1869 - Two-piece bolted urn, 16½″ tall, has original $7.50 price tag from Macy's, green mark #47

Plate 1871 - Covered urn, 13″ tall, similar to Plate 941, green mark #52

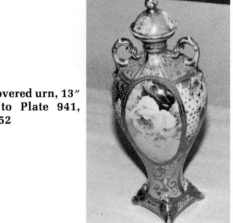

Plate 1872 - Two-piece bolted urn, 15½″ tall, green mark #47

Plate 1873 - Covered urn, 10″ tall, green mark #47

Plate 1874 - Two-piece bolted urn, 11¾" tall, green mark #52

Plate 1875 - Two-piece bolted urn, 12" tall, green mark #47

Plate 1876 - Two-piece bolted urn, 19½" tall, green mark #47

Plate 1877 - Pair of two-piece bolted urns, 12¼" tall, green mark #47

Plate 1878 - Urn, 16" tall, mark #47

Plate 1879 - Two-piece bolted urn, 16" tall, green mark #47

Plate 1880 - Pair of candle lamps, 15″ tall, base alone is 6¼″ tall, green mark #47

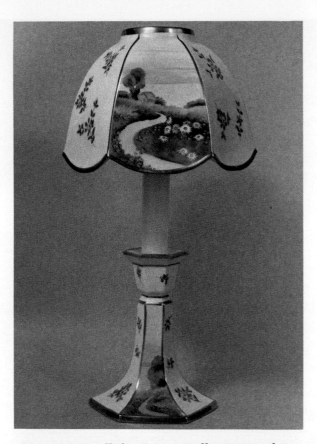

Plate 1881 - Candle lamp, 12¼″ tall, green mark #47

Plate 1882 - Pair of candle lamps, 12″ tall, green mark #47

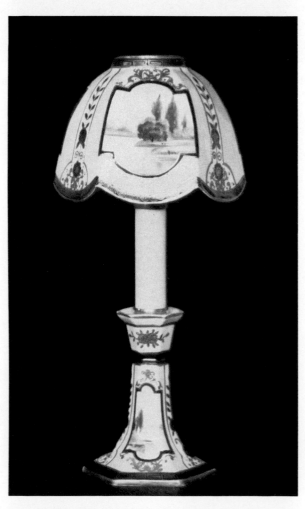

Plate 1883 - Candle lamp, 13″ tall, green mark #47

Plate 1885 - Lamp, 17″ tall to top of socket, green mark #52

Plate 1884 - Lamp with handpainted shade, 24″ tall, green mark #47

Plate 1886 - Lamp, base is 14½″ tall, blue mark #52

Plate 1887 - Lamp, base is 18″ tall, blue mark #52

226

Plate 1888 - Lamp, 17″ tall, mark unknown

Plate 1889 - Lamp, 21″ tall, incised with mark #55, has original price tag from Macy's

Plate 1890 - Lamp, 13½″ tall, green mark #47

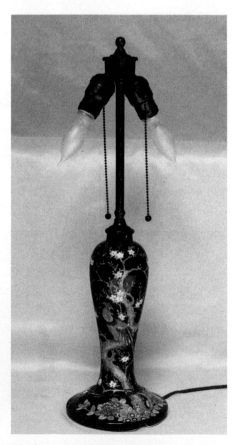

Plate 1891 - Lamp, 14½″ tall, mark unknown

Plate 1892 - Lamp, base is 8″ tall, mark #91

Plate 1893 - Lamp, porcelain base is 11½″ tall, mark #50

Plate 1894 - Humidor, 7″ tall, green mark #47

Plate 1895 - Humidor, 5″ tall, green mark #47

Plate 1896 - Humidor, 5½″ tall, green mark #47

Plate 1897 - Humidor, 6½″ tall, artist signed "Kakiyama", green mark #47

Plate 1898 - Humidor, 6¾″ tall, green mark #47

Plate 1899 - Humidor, 7½″ tall, green mark #47

Plate 1900 - Humidor, 5¾″ tall, green mark #47

Plate 1901 - Humidor, 4½″ tall, green mark #47

228

Plate 1902 - Humidor, 9¾″ tall, blue mark #47

Plate 1903 - Humidor, 7″ tall, blue mark #37

Plate 1904 - Humidor, 5½″ tall, green mark #47

Plate 1905 - Humidor, 5½″ tall, blue mark #52

Plate 1906 - Humidor, 5¾″ tall, green mark #47

Plate 1907 - Humidor, 4¾″ tall, green mark #47

Plate 1908 - Humidor, 7½″ tall, green mark #47

Plate 1909 - Humidor, 4½″ tall, green mark #47

229

Plate 1910 - Humidor, 6½″ tall, green mark #47

Plate 1911 - Humidor, 6″ tall, green mark #47

Plate 1912 - Humidor, 4½″ tall, green mark #47

Plate 1913 - Humidor, 6″ tall, green mark #47

Plate 1914 - Humidor, 6¼″ tall, green mark #47

Plate 1915 - Humidor, 6¼″ tall, green mark #47

Plate 1916 - Humidors, each 5½″ tall, green mark #47

230

Plate 1917 - Humidor, blue mark #38

Plate 1918 - Humidor, 6¾″ tall, green mark #47

Plate 1919 - Humidor, 7½″ tall, mark #47

Plate 1920 - Humidor, 5¾″ tall, green mark #47

Plate 1921 - Humidor, 6¾″ tall, green mark #47

Plate 1922 - Humidor, 5½″ tall, mark #52

Plate 1923 - Smoke set, tray is 10¾" long, humidor is 4¾" tall, green mark #47

Plate 1924 - Ashtray, 5" in diameter, green mark #47

Plate 1925 - Smoke set pieces, mark #47

Plate 1926 - Smoke set, tray is 10¾" long, green mark #47

Plate 1927 - Smoke set, tray is 7" in diameter, green mark #47

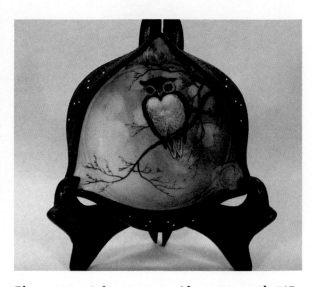

Plate 1928 - Ashtray, 5½" wide, green mark #47

Plate 1929 - Ashtray, 5¼″ wide, green mark #47

Plate 1930 - Smoke set, green mark #47

Plate 1931 - Smoke set, green mark #47

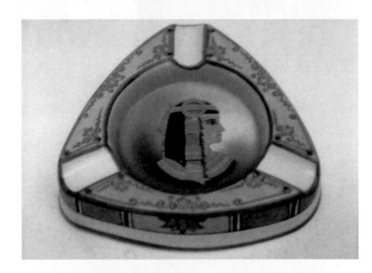

Plate 1932 - Ashtray, 4¾″ wide, mark #47

Plate 1933 - Combination matchbox holder and ashtray,
6½″ long, 3½″ tall, green mark #47

Plate 1934 - Smoke set, tray is 7″ in diameter, mark #47

Plate 1935 - Smoke set pieces, tray is 11″ wide, green mark #47

Plate 1936 - Cigarette box, 4½″ long, green mark #47

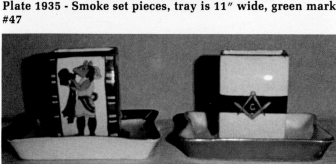

Plate 1937 - Combination matchbox holder and ashtrays, 3″ tall, 4″ wide; first has green mark #47, second has blue mark #68

Plate 1938 - Ashtray, 4¾″ wide, green mark #47

Plate 1939 - Smoke set, mark #47

Plate 1940 - Ashtrays, 5¼″ and 5″ wide, both green mark #47

Plate 1941 - Ashtray, 4½″ long, green mark #47

Plate 1942 - Smoke set, mark #47

Plate 1943 - Ashtray, 6½″ wide, blue mark #52

Plate 1944 - Smoke set, humidor, 5½″ tall, cigarette holder is 3½″ tall, ashtray, all have green mark #47

Plate 1945 - Ashtray, 5¼″ wide, green mark #47

Plate 1946 - Ashtray, 6″ tall, green mark #47

Plate 1947 - Ashtray and matchbox holder, 6½″ long, green mark #47

Plate 1948 - Ashtray, 5″ wide, green mark #47

Plate 1949 - Wine jug, 7½″ tall, blue mark #52

Plate 1950 - Wine jug, 9½″ tall, blue mark #52

Plate 1951 - Wine jug, 8½″ tall, green mark #47

Plate 1952 - Whiskey jug, 6½″ tall, green mark #47

Plate 1953 - Wine jug, 9½″ tall, green mark #47

Plate 1954 - Whiskey jug, 7½″ tall, blue mark #52

Plate 1955 - Whiskey jug, 5¾″ tall, mark #68

Plate 1956 - Whiskey jug, 6½″ tall, blue mark #52

236

Plate 1957 - Punch set, 16″ bowl sits on pedestal, set comes with 8 cups, green mark #47

Plate 1958 - Punch set, 13″ bowl sits on pedestal, set comes with 8 cups, green mark #47

Plate 1959 - Punch or large fruit bowl, 11″ wide, mark #47

Plate 1960 - Punch or large fruit bowl, 10″ wide, green mark #47

Plate 1961 - Punch or fruit bowl, 12¼″ across handles, green mark #47

Plate 1962 - Lobster plate, 8¾″ wide, green mark #52

Plate 1963 - Serving platter, 17½″ long, part of a game set, see Plates 1965, 1967 and 1968 for remainder of set, blue mark #52

Plate 1964 - Game plate, 9″ wide, green mark #52

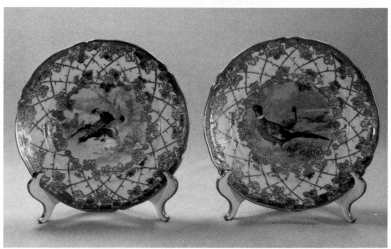

Plate 1965 - Game plates, 9″ wide, part of a game set, see Plates 1963, 1967 and 1968 for remainder of pieces, blue mark #52

Plate 1966 - Game plate, 9″ wide, unmarked

Plate 1967 - Game plates, 9″ wide, part of a game set shown in Plates 1963, 1965 and 1968, blue mark #52

Plate 1968 - Game plates, 9″ wide, part of game set shown in Plates 1963, 1965 and 1967, blue mark #52

Plate 1969 - Game platter, 16¾″ long, green mark #47

Plate 1970 - Fish plates, 8¾″ wide, see Plates 1971, 1972 and 1973 for matching pieces, green mark #52

Plate 1971 - Fish plates, 8¾″ wide, See Plates 1970, 1972, and 1973 for matching pieces, green mark #52

Plate 1972 - Fish platter, 17¼″ long, matches fish plates in Plates 1970, 1971 and 1973, green mark #52

Plate 1973 - Fish plates, 8¾″ wide, matches platter and other plates in Plates 1970, 1971 and 1972, green mark #52

Plate 1974 - Chocolate set, pot is 10″ tall, set has five cups and saucers, blue mark #52

Plate 1975 - Chocolate pot, 10″ tall, green mark #47

Plate 1976 - Chocolate pot, 14″ tall, blue mark #52

Plate 1977 - Chocolate set, pot is 12″ tall, mark #81

Plate 1978 - Chocolate set, comes with six cups and saucers, mark #52

Plate 1979 - Chocolate set, pot is 9″ tall, set comes with six cups and saucers, green mark #47

Plate 1981 - Chocolate set, pot is 9½″ tall, set comes with six cups and saucers, blue mark #87

Plate 1980 - Chocolate set, pot is 9¾″ tall, set comes with six cups and saucers, green mark #47

Plate 1982 - Chocolate set, pot is 9¾″ tall, mark #71

Plate 1983 - Chocolate pot, 9½″ tall, mark #7

Plate 1984 - Chocolate set, pot is 9″ tall, set comes with six cups and saucers, green mark #47

Plate 1985 - Chocolate set, pot is 9½″ tall, set comes with four cups and saucers, green mark #47

Plate 1986 - Chocolate pot, 9″ tall, green mark #47

Plate 1987 - Chocolate set, pot is 10″ tall, mark #81

Plate 1988 - Chocolate set, pot is 9″ tall, mark #81

Plate 1989 - Chocolate pot, 8½″ tall, mark scratched off; sugar and creamer, mark #73; cup and saucer, mark #52

Plate 1990 - Chocolate set, pot and four cups and saucers, trivet and serving tray, green mark #47

Plate 1991 - Chocolate set, pot is 10″ tall, set comes with six cups and saucers, green mark #47

Plate 1992 - Chocolate set, pot is 11″ tall, set comes with four cups and saucers, blue mark #52

Plate 1993 - Chocolate pot, 9″ tall, blue mark #52

Plate 1994 - Chocolate set, pot is 9½″ tall, compote is 5″ in diameter, blue mark #52

Plate 1995 - Tea set, teapot is 5″ tall, cookie jar is 6½″ tall, green mark #47

Plate 1996 - Tea set, blue mark #71, set comes with 6 cups & saucers

Plate 1997 - Two cup size teapot, 5″ tall, blue mark #52

Plate 1998 - Tea set, pot is 6″ tall, mark #110

Plate 1999 - Tea set, mark #89

Plate 2000 - Tea set, pot is 5″ tall, set comes with six cups and saucers, green mark #47

Plate 2001 - Tea set, pot is 5½″ tall, green mark #47

Plate 2002 - Tea pot, 5¼″ tall, mark #118

Plate 2003 - Tea set, pot is 5″ tall, blue mark #52

Plate 2004 - Tea set, pot is 4¾″ tall, green mark #52

Plate 2005 - Tea set, pot is 6″ tall, blue mark #52

Plate 2006 - Tea set complete with serving tray, green mark #47, set comes with 6 cups & saucers

Plate 2007 - Coffee pot, 8″ tall, blue mark #52

Plate 2008 - Coffee pot, individual size, 6¼″ tall, blue mark #52

Plate 2009 - Tea pot, 4¼″ tall, green mark #47

Plate 2010 - Tea set, pot is 7¾″ tall, set comes with six cups and saucers, mark #38

Plate 2011 - Demitasse set, green mark #47

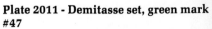

Plate 2012 - Demitasse set, pot is 6½″ tall, mark #91, set comes with 6 cups & saucers

Plate 2013 - Demitasse set, pot is 8½″ tall, mark #7

Plate 2014 - Demitasse set, pot is 6¼″ tall, green mark #47

Plate 2015 - Ferner, 5¾″ wide, mark #47

Plate 2016 - Ferner, 5¾″ wide, green mark #47

Plate 2017 - Ferner, 6½″ in diameter, green mark #47

Plate 2018 - Ferner, 5½″ tall, green mark #47

Plate 2019 - Ferner, 5½″ wide, green mark #47

Plate 2020 - Ferner, 7″ long, green mark #47

Plate 2021 - Ferner, 5½″ long on all three sides, green mark #47

Plate 2022 - Ferner, 8″ in diameter, green mark #47

Plate 2023 - Ferner, 5½″ wide, mark #89

Plate 2024 - Ferner, 8½″ wide, blue mark #52

Plate 2025 - Ferner with gold lion decoration, 5½″ long, mark #52

Plate 2026 - Pedestal ferner, 5½″ tall, green mark #47

251

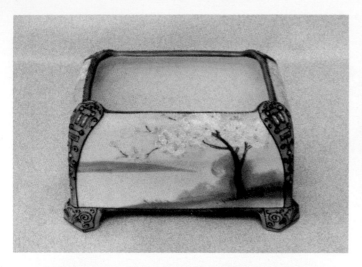

Plate 2027 - Ferner, 5¾″ long, blue mark #47

Plate 2028 - Ferner, 5¾″ long, green mark #47

Plate 2029 - Ferner, 5½″ wide, blue mark #52

Plate 2030 - Hanging ferner, 5″ long, green mark #47

Plate 2031a - Ferner, 7″ wide, mark #47

Plate 2031b - Rear view of ferner shown in Plate 2031a

Plate 2032 - Pair of candlesticks, 7¾" tall, green mark #47

Plate 2033 - Pair of candlesticks, 6¼" tall, mark #82

Plate 2034 - Chamberstick, green mark #47

Plate 2035 - Candlestick, 8" tall, green mark #47

Plate 2036a - Pair of candlesticks, 11½" tall, blue mark #52

Plate 2036b - Paper label found on pair of candlesticks shown in Plate 2036a; from Farrington, Importer of China in Poughkeepsie, N.Y.

Plate 2037 - Candlestick, 8″ tall, green mark #47

Plate 2038 - Candlestick, 7½″ tall, blue mark #47

Plate 2039 - Candlestick, 8″ tall, green mark #47

Plate 2040 - Tankard, 12¾″ tall, blue mark #52

Plate 2041 - Tankard, 13″ tall, mark #91

Plate 2042 - Ewer, 7½″ tall, blue mark #52

Plate 2043 - Pitcher, 7″ tall, green mark #47

Plate 2044 - Tankard, 14″ tall, mark #70

Plate 2045 - Pitcher, 6″ tall, blue mark #52

Plate 2046 - Ewer, 10″ tall, blue mark #52

Plate 2047 - Pitcher, 6½″ tall, mark #52

Plate 2048 - Beverage set, pitcher is 8½″ tall, mugs are 4″ tall, green mark #47, set comes with 6 mugs

Plate 2049 - Tankard, 10″ tall, mark #157

Plate 2050 - Pitcher, 7″ tall, blue mark #81

Plate 2051 - Beverage set, pitcher is 9½″ tall, tumblers are 4″ tall, green mark #47

Plate 2053 - Tankard set, tankard is 12″ tall, mugs are 4″ tall, mark #109

Plate 2052 - Tankard, 11″ tall, blue mark #47

Plate 2054 - Pitcher, 7″ tall, blue mark #92

Plate 2055 - Tankard, 12″ tall, large matching plate, 10″ wide, small plate, 7½″ wide, mark #38

Plate 2056 - Pitcher, 7″ tall, mark #52

Plate 2057 - Tankard, 10¼″ tall, mark #52

Plate 2058 - Ewer, 7½″ tall, blue mark #52

Plate 2059 - Covered pitcher, 5½″ tall, green mark #47

Plate 2060 - Covered pitcher, 5½″ tall, green mark #47

Plate 2061 - Stein, 7¼″ tall, blue mark #52

Plate 2062 - Mug, 5½″ tall, blue mark #47; mug, 5½″ tall, blue mark #4

Plate 2063 - Mug, 5″ tall, green mark #47

Plate 2064 - Mug, 5″ tall, mark #52; pitcher, 4″ tall, mark #47; mug, 5″ tall, blue mark #52

Plate 2065 - Mug, 5½″ tall, mark #47

Plate 2066 - Shaving mugs, each 3¾″ tall, green mark #47

258

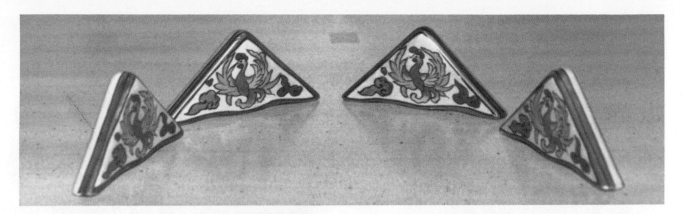

Plate 2067 - Blotter corners, 4″ long, green mark #47

Plate 2068 - Desk calendar, 3″ tall, 4½″ wide, green mark #47

Plate 2069 - Letter holder, 6″ long, 4½″ tall, green mark #47

Plate 2070 - Inkwell, 3″ tall, mark #47

Plate 2071 - Letter holder and matching roller blotter, mark #47

Plate 2072 - Inkwell with insert, 4″ tall, green mark #47

Plate 2073 - Inkwell, 4″ wide, mark #47

Plate 2074 - Inkwell, 2½″ long, green mark #47

Plate 2075 - Cracker or cookie jar, 7½″ tall, unmarked

Plate 2076 - Cracker jar, 5″ tall, 8″ in diameter, blue mark #52

Plate 2077 - Cracker jar, 8″ in diameter, blue mark #40

Plate 2078 - Cracker or cookie jar, 6½″ tall, green mark #47

Plate 2079 - Cracker or cookie jar, 7½″ tall, blue mark #52

Plate 2080 - Cracker jar, 9½″ wide, compote, 3½″ tall, both mark #47

Plate 2082 - Cracker jar, 9½″ across including handles, blue mark #52

Plate 2081 - Cracker or cookie jar, 7½″ tall, green mark #47

Plate 2083 - Master sugar bowl, 6½″ in diameter, magenta mark #47

Plate 2084 - Cracker or cookie jar, 9″ tall, mark #52

Plate 2085 - Cracker jar, 9″ across, green mark #47

Plate 2086 - Master sugar bowl, 6½″ wide, blue mark #52

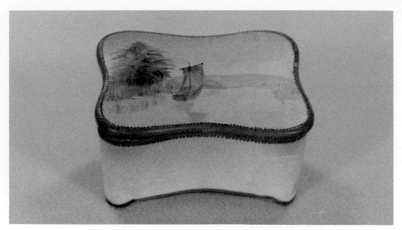

Plate 2088 - Trinket box, 3¼" long, green mark #47

Plate 2087 - Dresser set, tray is 11½", hatpin holder, 4¾" tall, pin dish is 4¼" wide, hair receiver and powder box are 3½" wide, green mark #47

Plate 2089 - Trinket box, 4" long, red mark #47

Plate 2090 - Hair receivers, 3" wide; left mark: #9, right mark: #84

Plate 2091 - Hair receiver, 4¾" wide; powder box, 4¼" wide; both have mark #52

Plate 2092 - Hatpin holder, 4¾" tall, mark #47

262

Plate 2093 - Hair receiver and powder box, both 4″ in diameter, green mark #47

Plate 2094 - Powder box, 5½″ in diameter, green mark #52

Plate 2095 - Hair receiver, 4½″ wide, green mark #52

Plate 2096 - Powder box, 2¾″ wide, mark #43; hair receiver, 3″ in diameter, green mark #47

Plate 2097 - Dresser tray, 10″ long, mark #4

Plate 2098 - Hatpin holder, 3½″ tall, mark #47

Plate 2099 - Hatpin holder, 4¾″ tall, green mark #47

Plate 2100 - Dresser tray, woodland scene, 11″ long, mark #47

Plate 2101 - Covered box, 3½″ wide, green mark #47

Plate 2102 - Hatpin holder, 5″ tall, green mark #47

Plate 2103 - Cologne bottle, 4¾″ tall, blue mark #52

Plate 2104 - Powder box, 3½″ in diameter, mark #84

Plate 2105 - Cologne bottle, 6″ tall, blue mark #47

Plate 2106 - Cologne bottle, 6″ tall, blue mark #52

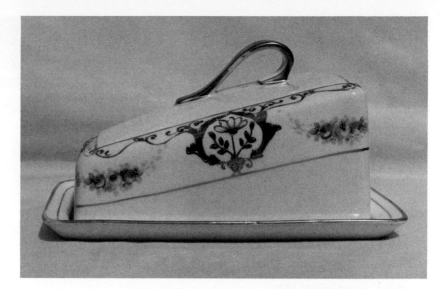

Plate 2108 - Slanted cheese dish, 7¾" long, blue mark #103

Plate 2107 - Tea caddy, 5" tall, blue mark #52

Plate 2109 - Sherbets, 4¾" tall, 3¾" in diameter, magenta mark #47; sherbets lift out of metal holders made by Manning Bowman, Meridan, Conn.

Plate 2110 - Slanted cheese dish, 7¾" long, mark #84

Plate 2111 - Covered jar, 7¾" tall, green mark #47

Plate 2112 - Potpourri jar, 6" tall, mark #52

Plate 2113 - Tea caddy, 4½" tall, mark #55

Plate 2114 - Juicer or reamer, 4½″ in diameter, green mark #47

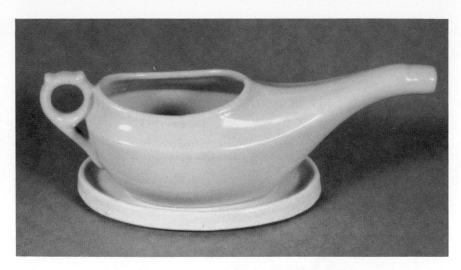

Plate 2115 - Invalid feeding dish, mark #55

Plate 2116 - Tea tile, 6¼″ wide, green mark #47

Plate 2117 - Egg warmer, 5″ wide, green mark #47

Plate 2118a - Stacked tea set, consists of teapot, tea tile, creamer and sugar, green mark #47

Plate 2118b - Same as Plate 2118a but shows items when they are not stacked

Plate 2120 - Potpourri jar with inner cover, 5¾″ tall, blue mark #52

Plate 2119 - Coasters, each 3¾″ wide, green mark #47

Plate 2121 - Honey pot, 5½″ tall, green mark #47

Plate 2122 - Perfume bottle, 4″ tall, loving cup, 4″ tall, green mark #47

Plate 2123 - Toast rack, 5″ long, mark #84

Plate 2124 - Loving cup, 3¾″ tall, mark #47

Plate 2125 - Condiment set, mustard pot, salt and pepper shakers, toothpick holder, tray, 7″ wide, green mark #47

Plate 2126 - Talcum flask, 4¾″ tall, mark #68

Plate 2127 - Egg warmer, 5½″ in diameter, blue mark #84

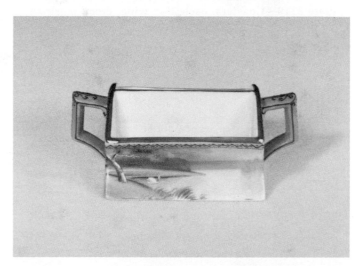

Plate 2128 - Double sugar cube holder, 5½″ long, green mark #47

Plate 2129 - Hanging double match box holder, 5″ long, green mark #47

Plate 2130 - Covered mug, 5¾″ tall, blue mark #52

Plate 2131 - Tumbler, 4″ tall, mark #7

Plate 2132 - Jam jar, 5″ tall, green mark #47

Plate 2133 - Tea strainer, blue mark #52

Plate 2134 - Condensed milk container, mark #80

Plate 2135 - Tea strainer, 4½″ long, green mark #47

Plate 2136 - Condensed milk container, 5½″ tall, green mark #81

Plate 2137 - Condensed milk container, 6″ tall, mark #79

Plate 2138 - Condensed milk container, 6″ tall, mark #52

Plate 2139 - Sweetmeat set, dishes come in black lacquered box which is 9½″ in diameter, blue mark #84

Plate 2140 - Sweetmeat set, 8½″ in diameter, mark #101

Plate 2141 - Sugar shaker, 5″ tall, blue mark #52

Plate 2142 - Sugar shaker, 5″ tall, mark #52; sugar shaker "muffineer", 5″ tall, green mark #47

Plate 2143 - Sugar shaker, 5¼″ tall, green mark #47

Plate 2144 - Cheese and cracker server, attached plate is 8″ wide, blue mark #84

Plate 2145 - Toothpick holder, 3″ tall, green mark #47

Plate 2146 - Celery set, master dish is 13½″ long, mark #87

Plate 2147 - Celery set, master dish is 13″ long, small salts are 3¾″ long, green mark #47

Plate 2148 - Toothpick holder, 2½″ tall, green mark #47

Plate 2149 - Toothpick holder, 2½″ tall, green mark #47

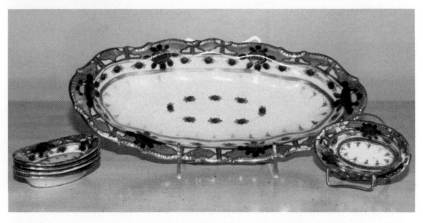

Plate 2150 - Celery set, master dish is 12″ long, salts are 3½″ long, mark #101

Plate 2151 - Celery set, master dish is 12″ long, salts are 3¾″ long, green mark #47

Plate 2152 - Toothpick holder, 2″ tall, mark #47

Plate 2153 - Celery set, master dish is 12½″ long, mark #84

Plate 2154 - Relish set, master dish is 8½″ long, salts are 3¾″ long, green mark #47

Plate 2155 - Celery set, dish is 12¼″ long, individual salts are 2½″ long, mark #84

Plate 2156 - Mustard pot, 3½″ tall, blue mark #52

Plate 2157 - Mustard pot, 4″ tall, green mark #47

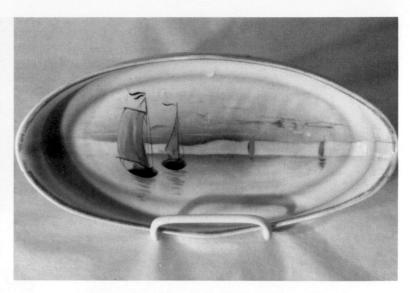

Plate 2158 - Celery dish, 9″ long, mark #52

Plate 2159 - Relish set, master dish and individual salts; a salt shaker in matching pattern, mark #52

Plate 2160 - Mustard pot, 3¼″ tall, blue mark #52

Plate 2161 - Nut set, master bowl is 8¾″ wide, small bowls are 2¾″ wide, green mark #47

Plate 2162 - Nut set, master bowl is 6½″ wide, small ones are 3″ wide, green mark #47

Plate 2163 - Nut set, master bowl is 6″ wide, individual bowls are 2¾″ wide, green mark #47

Plate 2164 - Nut set, large bowl is 6″ wide, small ones are 3″ wide, blue mark #84

Plate 2165 - Nut set, large bowl is 7¼″ wide, small ones are 2½″ wide, green mark #47

Plate 2166 - Serving dish, 9″ wide, green mark #47

Plate 2167 - Nut set, large bowl is 7¼″ wide, small ones are 2½″ wide, green mark #47

Plate 2168 - Serving dish, 8½″ wide, green mark #47

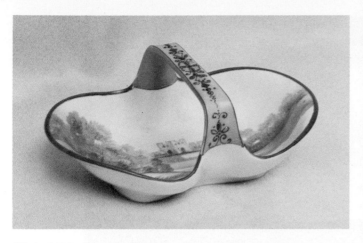

Plate 2169 - Handled serving dish, 8″ long, green mark #47

Plate 2170 - Three compartment dish, 7″ in diameter, blue mark #84

Plate 2171 - Three compartment dish, 7″ wide, green mark #47

Plate 2172 - Butter dish, bottom dish is 7″ wide, blue mark #52

Plate 2173 - Handled serving dish, 8¼″ long, green mark #47

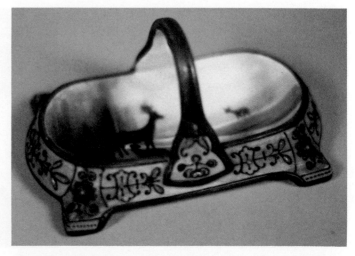

Plate 2174 - Handled calling card tray, 5½″ long, green mark #47

Plate 2175 - Ice cream set, tray is 12½″ long, green mark #47, set comes with 6 dishes

Plate 2177 - Master ice cream serving dish, 10½″ across handles, green mark #47

Plate 2176 - Bowl set, large bowl is 10½″ wide, set comes with six small bowls which are 5¼″ wide, red mark #47

Plate 2178 - Pierced berry bowl with underplate, bowl is 5¼″ across, blue mark #52

Plate 2179 - Ice cream set, tray is 12½″ long, small plates are 5½″ wide, green mark #47, set comes with 6 small plates

Plate 2181 - Pierced berry dish and underplate, bowl is 7½″ wide, mark #52

Plate 2180 - Bowl set, large bowl is 10½″ wide, set comes with six small bowls which are 5¼″ wide, red mark #47

Plate 2183 - Fruit set, tray is 12″ in diameter, compote is 9″ wide, green mark #47

Plate 2182 - Bowl set, large bowl is 10¼″ wide, small ones are 5¼″ wide, green mark #47

Plate 2184 - Pierced berry bowl, 5¼″ across, blue mark #52

Plate 2185 - Corn set, tray is 12″ long, small serving dishes are 7″ long, green mark #47

Plate 2186 - Bowl set, large bowl is 10½″ wide, set comes with six small bowls which are 5¼″ wide, red mark #47

Plate 2187 - Bouillon cup and saucer, cup is 4″ tall with cover, unmarked

Plate 2188 - Pierced berry dish and underplate, bowl is 7½″ wide, blue mark #52

Plate 2189 - Ice cream set, tray is 12½″ long, mark #80

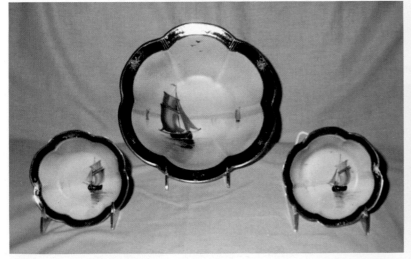

Plate 2190 - Berry set, master bowl is 9¾″ wide, comes with four smaller matching bowls which are 5¼″ wide, green mark #47

Plate 2191 - Compote, 10″ wide including handles, green mark #47

Plate 2193 - Compote, 7″ wide, blue mark #52

Plate 2192 - Compote, 7″ wide, mark #26

Plate 2194 - Compote, 7″ wide, blue mark #52

Plate 2195 - Compote, 11½″ wide, handle to handle, green mark #47

Plate 2196 - Pancake server, bottom piece is 8¾″ across, mark #180

Plate 2197 - Pancake server, mark #87

Plate 2198 - Pancake server, bottom dish is 8½″ wide, mark #84

Plate 2199 - Salt and pepper shakers, 3¼″ tall, mark #55

Plate 2200 - Pancake server, bottom dish is 8½″ wide, mark #68

Plate 2201 - Child's dish, 7″ wide, blue mark #84

Plate 2202 - Creamer, 4″ tall, mark #218

Plate 2203 - Salt and pepper shakers, first set has green mark #47, second set has mark #21

Plate 2204 - Two-tier dish, 9½″ wide, red mark #47

Plate 2205 - Two-tier dish, 9½″ wide, green mark #47

Plate 2206 - Soap dish, 7¼″ wide, blue mark #52

Plate 2207 - Tray, 9¾″ wide, blue mark #68

Plate 2208 - Child's mug, 3¾″ tall, blue mark #84

Plate 2209 - Bread tray, 17½″ long, green mark #47

Plate 2210 - Creamer and sugar bowl, sugar bowl is 4″ tall, green mark #47

Plate 2211 - Sugar bowl and creamer, blue mark #52

Plate 2212 - Creamer, 5½″ wide, sugar bowl, 6½″ wide, blue mark #30

Plate 2213 - Sugar and creamer set, sugar bowl is 4″ tall, creamer is 3″ tall, green mark #47

Plate 2214 - Sugar bowl and creamer, sugar bowl is 4¾″ tall, green mark #47

Plate 2215 - Sugar bowl and creamer, sugar bowl is 4½″ tall, mark #82

Plate 2216 - Sugar bowl and creamer, creamer is 3½″ tall, sugar bowl is 4½″ tall, blue mark #89

Plate 2217 - Plate, 9″ in diameter, blue mark #52

Plate 2218 - Platter, 13″ in diameter, blue mark #88

Plate 2219 - Plate, 10″ in diameter, mark #52

Plate 2221 - Serving tray, 14″ in diameter, blue mark #52

Plate 2220 - Plate, 7¼″ in diameter, blue mark #52

Plate 2222 - Platter, 15¾″ in diameter, green mark #47

Plate 2223 - Serving tray, 10½″ in diameter, blue mark #52

Plate 2224 - Serving tray, 11½″ in diameter, green mark #47

Plate 2225 - Serving tray, 10½″ wide, blue mark #52

Plate 2226 - Plate, 11″ in diameter, blue mark #52

Plate 2227 - Plate, 10½″ in diameter, gold overlay trim, green mark #47

Plate 2228 - Plate, 7½″ in diameter, green mark #47

Plate 2229 - Plate, 7¾″ in diameter, green mark #47

Plate 2230 - Plate, 7¾″ in diameter, green mark #47

Plate 2231 - Plate, 6½″ in diameter, mark #10

Plate 2232 - Plate, 8½″ in diameter, blue mark #52

285

Plate 2233 - Cake plate, 10½″ in diameter, mark #89

Plate 2234 - Serving tray, 13½″ wide, mark #26

Plate 2235 - Cake plate, 10½″ in diameter, green mark #47

Plate 2236 - Cake plate, 11″ in diameter, green mark #47

Plate 2237 - Plate, 10″ in diameter, mark #52

Plate 2238 - Plate, 6½″ in diameter, mark #177

Plate 2239 - Serving plate, 9″ wide, green mark #47

Plate 2240 - Plate, 7½″ in diameter, green mark #47

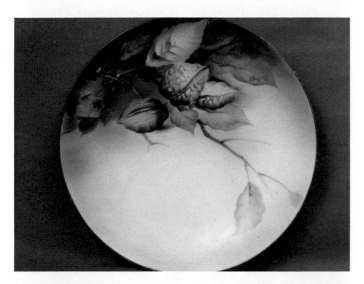

Plate 2241 - Plate, 7½″ in diameter, green mark #47

Plate 2242 - Plate, 7½″ in diameter, mark #7

Plate 2243 - Plate, 8¾″ in diameter, mark #6

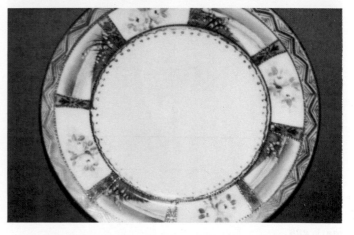

Plate 2244 - Plate, 7⅜″ in diameter, mark #99

Plate 2245 - Plate, 6½″ in diameter, mark #52

Plate 2246 - Plate, 8½″ in diameter, mark #40

Plate 2247 - Cake plate, 9½″ in diameter, mark #93

Plate 2248 - Plate, 6¼″ in diameter, green mark #47

Plate 2249 - Plate, 7¾″ in diameter, cup and saucer, green mark #66

Plate 2250 - Cup, green mark #47

Plate 2251 - Cake plate, 10½″ in diameter, mark #92

Plate 2252 - Plate, 6½″ in diameter, mark #10

Plate 2253 - Plate, 7½″ in diameter, mark #4

Plate 2254 - Cup and saucer, green mark #47

Plate 2255 - Cup and saucer, blue mark #52

Plate 2256 - Sugar and creamer, nappy which is 6¼″ wide, footed bowl is 6¼″ wide, all green mark #47

Plate 2257 - Bowl, 6¾″ wide, mark #52

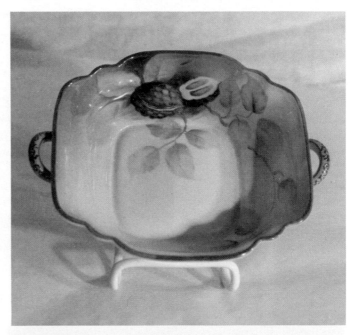

Plate 2258 - Bowl, 7½″ wide, green mark #47

Plate 2259 - Bowl, 5½″ wide, green mark #47

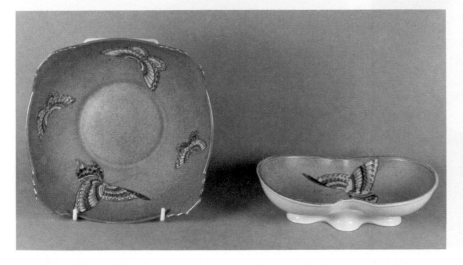

Plate 2260 - Bowl, 8″ in diameter, bowl 5″x7″, both green mark #47

Plate 2261 - Bowl, 9½″ in diameter, mark #52

Plate 2262 - Three footed bowl, 7¼″ wide, green
mark #47

Plate 2263 - Bowl, 8½″ wide, green mark #47

Plate 2264 - Bowl, 7¼″ across, blue mark #52

Plate 2265 - Bowl, 8½″ wide, green mark #47

Plate 2266 - Bowl, 6″ wide, no mark; bowl, 8″ wide, blue mark #4

Plate 2267 - Bowl, 7½″ wide, green
mark #47

291

Plate 2269 - Candy dish, green mark #47

Plate 2268 - Bowl, 6″ tall, green mark #47

Plate 2270 - Bowl, 6″ wide, Egyptian decor, green mark #47

Plate 2271 - Bowl, 7″ wide, green mark #47

Plate 2272 - Bowl, 7½″ long, green mark #47

Plate 2273 - Bowl, 9″ in diameter, green mark #47

Plate 2274 - Bowl, 6″ wide, green mark #47

Plate 2275 - Bowl, 7″ wide, mark #4

Plate 2276 - Bowl, 7½″ wide, green mark #47

Plate 2277 - Bowl, 6¾″ wide, green mark #47

Plate 2278 - Bowl, 11½″ wide including handles, green mark #47

Plate 2279 - Bowl, 10½″ long, green mark #47

Plate 2280 - Nut bowls, 6″ wide and 5″ wide, both green mark #47

Plate 2281 - Bowl, 6¾″ in diameter, green mark #47

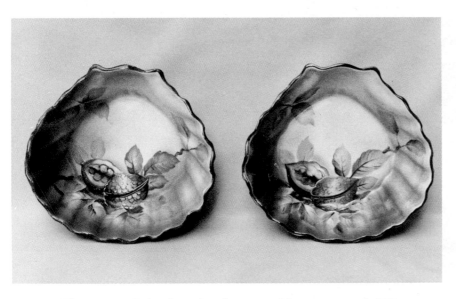

Plate 2282 - Pair of nut bowls, 6½″ wide, green mark #47

Plate 2283 - Bowl, 10¾″ wide, green mark #47

Plate 2284 - Bowls, both 6½″ wide, both green mark #47

Plate 2285 - Bowl, 8″ in diameter, green mark #52

294

Plate 2286 - Bowl, 7¼″ wide, green mark #47

Plate 2287 - Bowl, 8½″ wide, green mark #47

Plate 2288 - Bowl, 6″ wide, green mark #47

Plate 2289 - Bowl, 8¼″ long, green mark #47

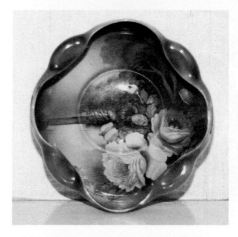

Plate 2290 - Bowl, 8″ wide, mark #47

Plate 2291 - Bowls, both 5¾″ long, both green mark #47

Plate 2292 - Bowl, 9¾″ wide, green mark #47

Plate 2293 - Bowl, 6½″ wide, green mark #47

Plate 2294 - Bowl, 5¾″ wide, mark #82

Plate 2295 - Bowl, 7¼″ long, mark #79

Plate 2296 - Bowl, 8″ wide, green mark #47

Plate 2297 - Bowl, 8¾″ wide, mark #80

Plate 2298 - Bowl, 5½″ across including handles, green mark #47

Plate 2300 - Bowl, 7½″ wide, green mark #47

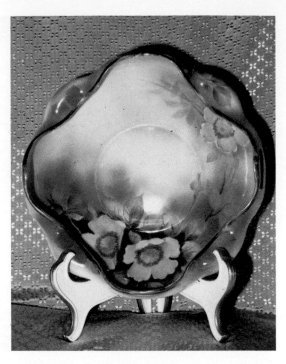

Plate 2299 - Bowl, 7½″ wide, green mark #47

Plate 2301 - Bowl, 6½″ wide, mark #47

Plate 2302 - Bowl, 9½″ wide, green mark #47

Plate 2303 - Bowl, 7½″ across, green mark #47

Plate 2304 - Bowl, 12″ wide, blue mark #52

Plate 2305 - Bowl, 9½″ wide, blue mark #52

Plate 2306 - Basket dish, 5¾″ wide, blue mark #52

Plate 2307 - Bowl, 7½″ wide, blue mark #52

Plate 2308 - Bowl, 8½″ in diameter, blue mark #52

Plate 2309 - Bowl, 7½″ across handles, mark #52

Plate 2310 - Footed bowl, 5½″ in diameter, 5″ tall, green mark #47

Plate 2311 - Bowl, 8½″ wide, blue mark #52

Plate 2312 - Nappy, 5″ wide, green mark #52

Plate 2313 - Bowl, 8½″ wide, mark #55

Plate 2314 - Bowl, 7¼″ in diameter, green mark #47

Plate 2315 - Bowl, 11½″ across, green mark #47

Plate 2316 - Top: left, bowl, 10″ wide; right, bowl, 9¼″ wide. Bottom: left, bowl 6¾″ wide; right, relish dish, 9″ long. All have green mark #47

Plate 2317 - Bowl, 5¾″ across, mark #7

Plate 2318 - Bowl, 9¾″ wide, mark #55

Plate 2319 - Bowl, 7½″ wide, mark #4

Plate 2320 - Bowl, 10″ across including handles, green mark #47

Plate 2322 - Doll, 27″ tall, ball-jointed composition body, brown sleep eyes, mark #183

Plate 2321 - Doll, 11″ tall, composition body, mark #171

Plate 2323 - Doll, 18″ tall, mark #152

Plate 2324 - Doll, 19″ tall, mark #154

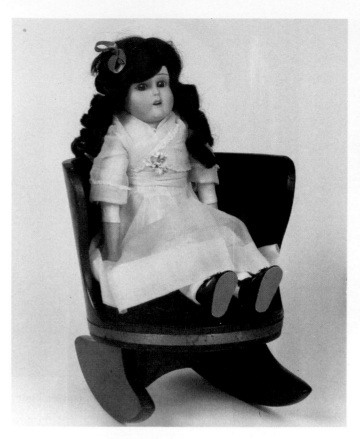

Plate 2325 - Doll, 22″ tall, mark #124

Plate 2326 - Doll, 21″ tall, toddler ball-jointed body, glass eyes, mark #163

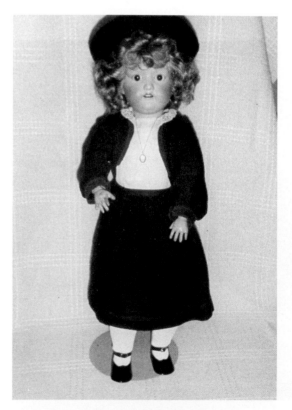

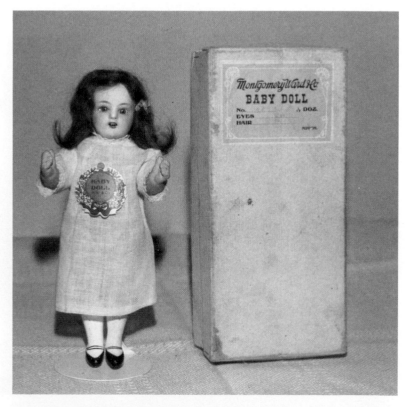

Plate 2327 - Doll, 24″ tall, ball-jointed composition body, brown sleep eyes, mark #168

Plate 2328 - Doll, 9″ tall, toddler, composition body with painted shoes and socks, blue sleep eyes, has original sticker mark #41; photo shows original Montgomery Ward & Co. box in which doll came packaged

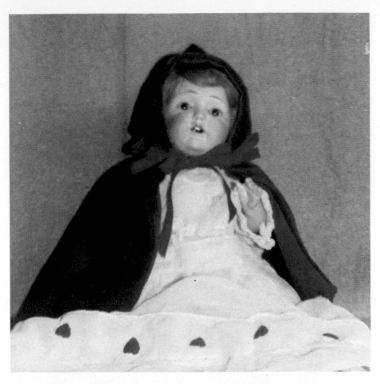

Plate 2329 - Doll, 10" tall, composition body, open/close eyes, mark #170

Plate 2330 - Doll, 13" tall, toddler composition body, brown sleep eyes, mark #198

Plate 2331 - Doll, 15" tall, ball-jointed composition body, blue eyes, mark #210

Plate 2332 - Doll, 12" tall, composition body, mark #153

Plate 2333 - Doll, 21″ tall, "Hilda", original mohair wig, glass eyes, composition body, mark #214

Plate 2334 - Doll, 21″ tall, mark #176

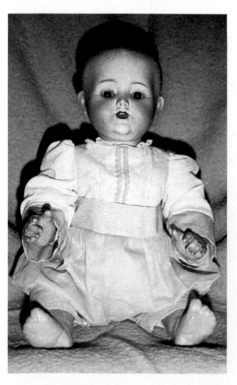

Plate 2335 - Doll, 21″ tall, mark #209

Plate 2336 - Doll, 11″ tall, composition body, glass eyes, mark #171

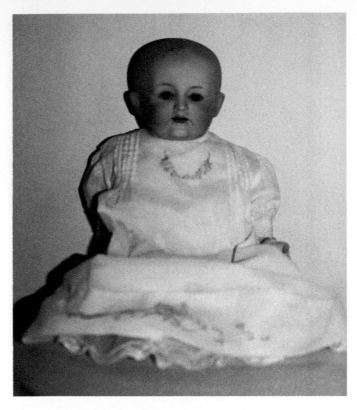

Plate 2337 - Doll, 18″ tall, mark #169

Plate 2338 - Doll, 15″ tall, papier mache baby body, blue sleep eyes, mark #215

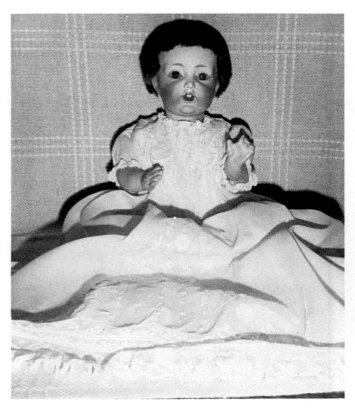

Plate 2339 - Doll, 13″ tall, composition baby body, brown sleep eyes, mark #172

Plate 2340 - Doll, 18″ tall, bisque shoulder plate, cloth body with bisque arms, blue sleep eyes, mark #172

Plate 2341 - Doll, 16″ tall, ball-jointed composition body, blue sleep eyes, mark #182

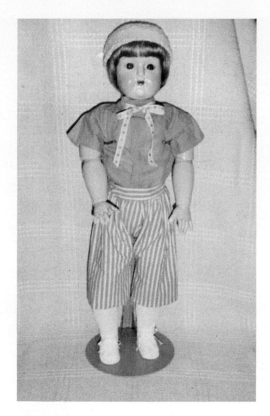

Plate 2342 - Doll, 27″ tall, doll has ball-jointed body, blue sleep eyes, unusual pale, oily bisque finish, mark #183

Plate 2343a - Doll, 22″ tall, mark #168

Plate 2343b - Close-up of doll shown in Plate 2343a

Plate 2344 - Doll, 24″ tall, ball-jointed body, open/close eyes, mark #168

Plate 2345 - Doll, 22″ tall, ball-jointed body, mark #168

Plate 2346 - Doll, 11½″ tall, composition baby body, blue sleep eyes, mark #212

Plate 2347 - Doll, 10″ tall, composition baby body, blue glass eyes, solid dome head with painted hair, unusual open-closed mouth with painted tongue and teeth, mark #186

Plate 2348 - Dolls, 7½" tall, mark #55

Plate 2349 - Doll, 6" tall, mark #55

Plate 2351 - Pincushion doll with bisque head, 3¾" tall, pink silk body with hand-painted arms and feet, mark #187

Plate 2350 - Doll, 6" tall, mark #55

Plate 2352 - Dolls, both 4¾" tall, mark #55

Plate 2353 - Dolls, both 7" tall, jointed arms and legs, painted shoes and socks, mark #55

Plate 2354 - Dolls, both are 4¾" tall, mark #55

Plate 2355 - Doll, 4¼″ tall, mark #55

Plate 2356 - Doll, 4¼″ tall, similar to Plate 135 only larger, mark #55

Plate 2357 - Doll, 5″ tall, mark #55

Plate 2358 - Doll, Indian maiden with frog at her feet, 4″ tall, mark #55

Plate 2359 - Pair of Happifats, girl has original sticker plus mark #55; boy has mark #55, 3½″ tall

Plate 2360 - Doll, 6″ tall, mark #55

Plate 2359b - Rear view of dolls shown in plate 2359a

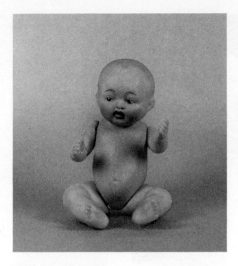

Plate 2361 - Doll, 4¾″ tall, mark #55

Plate 2362 - Doll, 6¼″ tall, mark #166

Plate 2363 - Doll with bottle, 3¾″ tall, mark #55

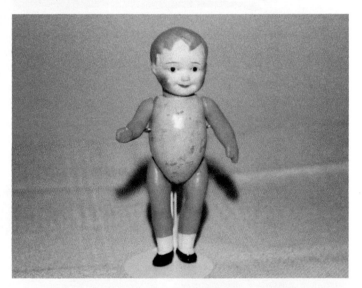

Plate 2364 - Doll, 5¾″ tall, mark #55

Plate 2365 - Doll, 8″ tall, composition body with painted shoes and socks, mark #55

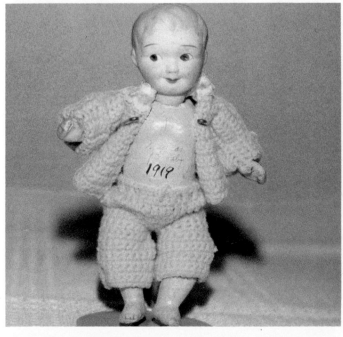

Plate 2366 - Doll, 7″ tall, composition body, writing on body says "Maude's 1st Baby 1919", mark #55

Plate 2367 - Doll, 5″ tall, mark #55

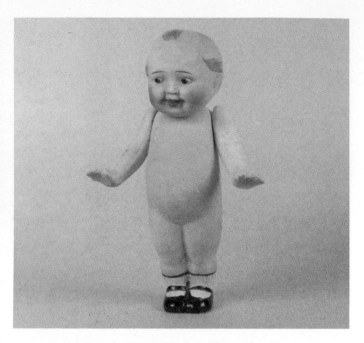

Plate 2368 - Bride and groom bisque dolls, 6″ tall, came from 1893 wedding cake, mark #55

Plate 2369 - Doll, 7″ tall, mark #55

Plate 2370 - Doll, 4¾″ tall, mark #55

Plate 2371a - "Manikin" doll, 3½″ tall, matches "Ladykin", has original sticker plus mark #55

Plate 2371b - Rear view of Plate 2371a showing sticker

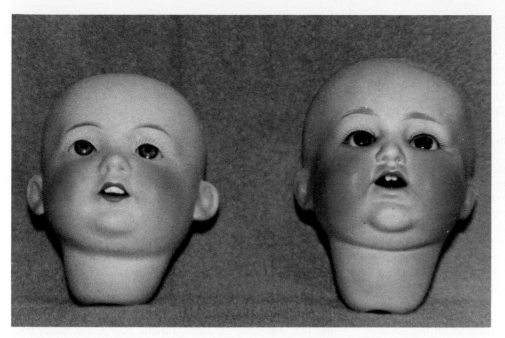

Plate 2372 - Doll head, 9½" in circumference, mark #175; doll head, 10½" in circumference, mark #213

Plate 2373 - Doll, 6½" tall, 8½" tall with dress which has six crepe paper layers supporting the doll, all original crepe paper clothes including parasol, mark #55

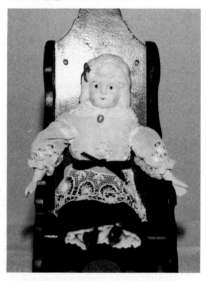

Plate 2374 - Red Riding Hood bisque doll, 4" tall, mark #55

Plate 2375 - Doll, 4" tall, baseball player, mark #55

Plate 2376 - Doll, 13" tall, "turned head" shoulder plate, red cloth body with bisque arms and legs, mark #55

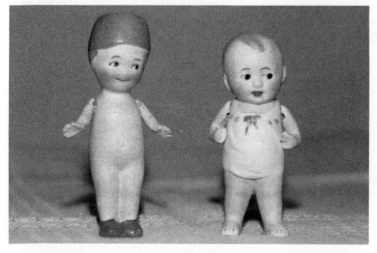

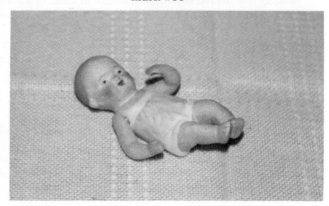

Plate 2377 - Doll, 4" tall, mark #55; doll 3¾" tall, mark #55

Plate 2378 - Doll, 5½" long, jointed arms, unusual piano baby, made to lay flat on back with legs raised in air, mark #55

313

GLOSSARY

American Indian design — a popular collectible in Nippon porcelain, these designs include the Indian in a canoe, Indian warrior, Indian hunting wild game and the Indian maiden.

Apricot (ume) — in Japan, stands for strength and nobility, is also a symbol of good luck.

Art Deco — a style of decoration which hit its peak in Europe and America around 1925 although items were manufactured with this decor as early as 1910. The style was modernistic; geometric patterns were popular. Motifs used were shapes such as circles, rectangles, cylinders and cones.

Art Nouveau — the name is derived from the French words meaning "new art." During the period of 1885-1925, artists tended to use bolder colors, and realism was rejected. Free-flowing designs were used, breaking away from the imitations of the past.

Artist signed — items signed by the artist, most appear to be of English extraction probably painted during the heyday of hand painting chinaware at the turn of the century.

Azalea pattern — pattern found on Nippon items, pink azaleas with green to gray leaves and gold rims. Nippon marked pieces match the Noritake marked azalea pattern items. The Azalea pattern was originally offered by the Larkin Co. to its customers as premiums.

Backstamp — mark found on Nippon porcelain items identifying the manufacturer, exporter or importer and country of origin.

Bamboo tree — in Japan, symbolic of strength, faithfulness and honesty, also a good luck symbol. The bamboo resists the storm but it yields to it and rises again.

Beading — generally a series of clay dots applied on Nippon porcelain, very often enameled over in gold. Later Nippon pieces merely had dots of enameling.

Bisquit — clay which has been fired but unglazed.

Bisque — same as biscuit, term also used by collectors to describe a matte finish on an item.

Blank — greenware of bisque items devoid of decoration.

Blown-out items — this term is used by collectors and dealers for items that have a molded relief pattern embossed on by the mold in which the article was shaped. It is not actually "blown-out" as glass items are, but the pattern is raised up from the background of the item. (See Molded Relief)

Bottger, Johann F. — a young German alchemist who supposedly discovered the value of kaolin in making porcelain. This discovery helped to revolutionize the china making industry in Europe beginning in the early 1700's.

Carp — fish that symbolizes strength and perseverance.

Casting — the process of making reproductions by pouring slip into molds.

Cha no yu - Japanese tea ceremony.

Chargers - archaic term for large platters or plates.

Cheese hard clay — same as leather hard clay.

Cherry blossoms — national flower of Japan and emblem of the faithful warrior.

Ching-te-Chen — ancient city in China where nearly a million people lived and worked with almost all devoted to the making of porcelain.

Chrysanthemum — depicts health and longevity, the crest of the Emperor of Japan. The chrysanthemum blooms late in the year and lives longer than other flowers.

Citron - stands for wealth.

Cloisonne' on Porcelain — on Nippon porcelain wares it resembles the other cloisonne' pieces except that it was produced on a porcelain body instead of metal. The decoration is divided into cells called cloisons. These cloisons were divided by strips of metal wire which kept the colors separated during the firing.

Cobalt oxide — blue oxide imported to Japan after 1868 for decoration of wares. Gosu, a pebble found in Oriental riverbeds had previously been used but was scarce and more expensive than the imported oxide. Cobalt oxide is the most powerful of all the coloring oxides for tinting.

Coralene items — were made by firing small colored beads on the wares. Most are signed Kinran, US Patent, NBR 912171, February 9, 1909, Japan. Tiny glass beads had previously been applied to glass items in the shapes of birds, flowers, leaves, etc. and no doubt this was an attempt to copy it. Japanese coralene was patented by Alban L. Rock, an American living in Yokohama, Japan. The vitreous coating of beads gave the item a plush velvety look. The beads were permanently fired on and gave a luminescence to the design. The most popular design had been one of seaweed and coral, hence the name coralene was given to this type of design.

Crane — a symbol of good luck in Japan, also stands for marital fidelity and is an emblem of longevity.

Daffodil — a sign of spring to the Japanese.

Decalcomania — a process of transferring a wet paper print onto the surface of an item. It was made to resemble hand painted work.

Deer — stands for divine messenger.

Diaper pattern — repetitive pattern of small design used on Nippon porcelain, often geometric or floral.

Dragons (ryu) — a symbol of strength, goodness and good fortune. The Japanese dragon has three claws and was thought to reside in the sky. Clouds, water and lightening often accompany the dragon. The dragon is often portrayed in high relief using the slip trailing method of decor.

Drain mold — a mold used in making hollow ware. Liquid slip is poured into the mold until the desired thickness of the walls is achieved. The excess clay is poured out. When the item starts to shrink away from the mold, it is removed.

Drape mold — or flopover mold, used to make flat bottomed items. Moist clay is rolled out and draped over the mold. It is then pressed firmly into shape.

Dutch scenes — popular on Nippon items, include those of windmills, and men and women dressed in Dutch costumes.

Edo — or Yedo, the largest city in Japan, later renamed Tokyo, meaning eastern capitol.

Embossed design — see molded relief.

Enamel beading — dots of enamling painted by the artist in gold or other colors and often made to resemble jewels such as emeralds and rubies. Many times this raised beading will be found in brown or black colors.

Fairings — items won or bought at fairs as souvenirs.

Feldspar — most common rock found on earth.

Fern Leaves — symbolic of ample good fortune.

Fettles or Mold Marks — ridges formed where sections of molds are joined at the seam. These fettles have to be removed before the item is decorated.

Finial — the top knob on a cover of an item, used to lift the cover off.

Firing — the cooking or baking of clay ware.

Flopover mold — same as drape mold.

Flux — an ingredient added to glaze to assist in making the item fire properly. It causes the glaze to melt at a specified temperature.

Glaze — composed of silica, alumina and flux, and is applied to porcelain pieces. During the firing process, the glaze joins together with the clay item to form a glasslike surface. It seals the pores and makes the item impervious to liquids.

Gold trim — has to be fired at lower temperatures or the gold would sink into the enameled decoration. If overfired, the gold becomes discolored.

Gouda ceramics — originally made in Gouda, a province of South Holland. These items were copies on the Nippon wares and were patterned after the Art Nouveau style.

Gosu — pebble found in Oriental riverbeds, a natural cobalt. It was used to color items until 1868 when oxidized cobalt was introduced into Japan.

Greenware — clay which has been molded but not fired.

Hard paste porcelain — paste meaning the body of substance, porcelain being made from clay using kaolin. This produces a hard translucent body when fired.

Ho·o bird — sort of a bird of paradise who resides on earth and is associated with the Empress of Japan. Also see phoenix bird.

Incised backstamp — the backstamp marking is scratched into the surface of a clay item.

Incised decoration — a sharp tool or stick was used to produce the design right onto the body of the article while it was still in a state of soft clay.

Iris — the Japanese believe this flower wards off evil; associated with warriors because of its sword-like leaves.

Jasper Ware — see Wedgwood.

Jigger — a machine resembling a potter's wheel. Soft pliable clay is placed onto a convex revolving mold. As the wheel turns, a template is held against it, trimming off the excess clay on the outside. The revolving mold shapes the inside of the item and the template cuts the outside.

Jolley — a machine like a jigger only in reverse. The revolving mold is concave and the template forms the inside of the item. The template is lowered inside the revolving mold. The mold forms the outside surface while the template cuts the inside.

Jomon — neolithic hunters and fishermen in Japan dating back to approximately 2500 B.C. Their pottery was hand formed and marked with an overall rope or cord pattern. It was made of unwashed clay, unglazed and was baked in open fires.

Kaga — province in Japan.

Kaolin — highly refractory clay and one of the principal ingredients used in making porcelain. It is a pure white residual clay, a decomposition of granite.

Kao-ling — Chinese word meaning "the high hills", the word kaolin is derived from it.

Kiln — oven in which pottery is fired.

Leather hard clay — clay which is dry enough to hold its shape but still damp and moist, no longer in a plastic state, also called cheese hard.

Liquid slip — clay in a liquid state.

Lobster — symbol of long life.

Luster decoration — a metallic type of coloring decoration, gives an irridescent effect.

Matte finish — also referred to as mat and matt. A dull glaze having a low reflectance when fired.

McKinley Tariff Act of 1890 — Chapter 1244, Section 6 states "That on and after the first day of March, eighteen hundred and ninety-one, all articles of foreign manufacture, such as are usually or ordinarily marked, stamped, branded, or labeled, and all packages containing such or other imported articles, shall, respectively, be plainly marked, stamped, branded, or labeled in legible English words, so as to indicate the country of their origin; and unless so marked, stamped, branded, or labeled, they shall not be admitted to entry."

Meiji perid — period of 1868 to 1912 in Japan when Emperor Mutsuhito reigned. It means "enlightened rule".

Middle East scenes — design used on Nippon pieces, featuring pyramids, deserts, palm trees and riders on camels.

Model — the shape from which the mold is made.

Molded relief items — the pattern is embossed on the item by the mold in which the article is shaped. These items give the appearance that the pattern is caused by some type of upward pressure from the underside. Collectors often refer to these items as "blown-out".

Molds — contain a cavity in which castings are made. They are generally made from plaster of paris and are used for shaping clay objects. Both liquid and plastic clay may be used. The mold can also be made of clay or rubber, however, plaster was generally used as it absorbed moisture immediately from the clay. Raised ornamentation may also be formed directly in the mold.

Moriage — refers to applied clay (slip) relief decoration. On Nippon items this was usually done by 'slip trailing' or hand rolling and shaping the clay on an item.

Morimura Bros. — importers of Japanese wares in the United States and the sole importers of Noritake wares. It was opened in New York City in 1876 and closed in 1941.

Mutsuhito — Emperor of Japan from 1868 to 1912. His reign was called the Meiji period which meant enlightened rule.

Nagoya — a large city in Japan.

Narcissus — stands for good fortune.

Ningyo — Japanese name for doll, meaning human being and image.

Nippon — the name the Japanese people called their country. It comes from a Chinese phrase meaning "the source of the sun" and sounds like Neehon in Japanese.

Noritake Co. — originally registered as Nippon Gomei Kaisha. In 1917 the name was changed to Nippon Toki Kabushiki Toki. From 1918 the word Noritake appeared in conjunction with Nippon which was the designation of country of origin.

Orchid — means hidden beauty and modesty to the Japanese.

Overglaze decoration — a design is either painted or a decal applied to an item which already has a fired glazed surface. The article is then refired to made the decoration permanent.

Pattern stamping — the design was achieved by using a special stamp or a plaster roll having the design cut into it. The design was pressed into the soft clay body of an item.

Panch — drink originating in India consisting of lemon juice, arrack, tea, sugar and water.

Paulownia flower — crest of the Empress of Japan.

Peach — stands for marriage.

Peacock — stands for elegance and beauty.

Peony — considered the king of flowers in Japan.

Perry, Matthew, Comm., USN — helped to fashion the Kanagawa treaty in 1854 between the United States and Japan. This treaty opened the small ports of Shimoda and Hakodate to trade. Shipwrecked sailors were also to receive good treatment and an American Consul was permitted to reside at Shimoda.

Petuntse — clay found in felspathic rocks such as granite. Its addition to porcelain made the item more durable. Petuntse is also called china stone.

Phoenix bird — sort of bird of paradise which resides on earth and is associated with the Empress of Japan. This bird appears to be a cross between a peacock, a pheasant and a gamecock. There appear to be many designs for this bird as each artist had his own conception as to how it should look. It is also a symbol to the Japanese of all that is beautiful.

Pickard Co. — a china decorating studio originally located in Chicago. This firm decorated blank wares imported from a number of countries including Nippon.

Pine tree — to the Japanese this tree is symbolic of friendship and prosperity and depicts the winter season. It is also a sign of good luck and a sign of strength.

Plastic clay — clay in a malleable state, able to be shaped and formed without collapsing.

Plum — stands for womanhood. Plum blossoms reflect bravery.

Porcelain — a mixture composed mainly of kaolin and petuntse which are fired at a high temperature and vitrified.

Porcelain slip — porcelain clay in a liquid form.

Porcellaine — French adaptation of the word porcelain.

Porcellana — Italian word meaning cowry shell. The Chinese ware which was brought back to Venice in the 15th century was thought to resemble the cowry shell and was called porcellana.

Portrait items — items decorated with portraits, many of Victorian ladies. Some appear to be hand painted, others are decal work.

Potter's wheel — rotating device onto which a ball of plastic clay is placed. The wheel is turned and the potter molds the clay with his hands and is capable of producing cylindrical objects.

Pottery — in its broadest sense, includes all forms of wares made from clay.

Press mold — used to make handles, finials, figurines, etc. A two-piece mold into which soft clay is placed. The two pieces are pressed together to form items.

Relief — molded (See Molded Relief Items).

Royal Ceramics — name of Nippon pieces marked with RC on backstamp.

Satsuma — a sea-going principality in Japan, an area where many of the old famous kilns are found, and also a type of Japanese ware. Satsuma is a cream colored glazed pottery which is finely crackled.

Slip — liquid clay.

Slip trailing — a process where liquid clay was applied to porcelain via a bamboo or rubber tube. A form of painting but with clay instead of paint. The slip is often applied quite heavily and gives a thick, raised appearance.

Slurry — thick slip.

Solid casting mold — used for shallow type items such as bowls and plates. In this type of mold, the thickness of the walls is determined by the mold and every piece is formed identical. The mold shapes both the inside and the outside of the piece and the thickness of the walls can be controlled. Solid casting can be done with either liquid or plastic clay.

Sometsuke style decoration — items decorated with an underglaze of blue and white colors.

Sprigging — the application of small molded relief decoration to the surface of porcelain by use of liquid clay as in Jasper Ware.

Sprig mold — a one-piece mold used in making ornaments. Clay is fitted or poured onto a mold which is incised with a design. Only one side is molded and the exposed side becomes the back of the finished item.

Taisho — name of the period reigned over by Emperor Yoshihito in Japan from 1912 to 1926. It means "great peace."

Tapestry — a type of decor used on Nippon porcelain. A cloth was dipped into liquid slip and then stretched onto the porcelain item. During the bisque firing the material burned off and left a textured look on the porcelain piece resembling needlepoint in many cases. The item was then painted and fired again in the usual manner.

Template — profile of the pattern being cut.

Throwing — the art of forming a clay object on a potter's wheel.

Tiger (tora) — a symbol of longevity.

Transfer print — see Decalcomania.

Translucent — not transparent but clear enough to allow rays of light to pass through.

Ultra violet lamp — lamp used to detect cracks and hidden repairs in items.

Underglaze decoration — this type of decoration is applied on bisque china (fired once), then the item is glazed and fired again.

Victorian Age design — decor used on some Nippon pieces, gaudy and extremely bold colors used

Vitreous — glass-like.

Vitrify — to change into a glasslike substance due to the application of heat.

Wasters — name given to pieces ruined or marred in the kiln.

Water lilies — represents autumn in Japan.

Wedgwood — term used to refer to Nippon pieces which attempt to imitate Josiah Wedgwood's Jasper Ware. The items generally have a light blue or green background. The Nippon pieces were produced with a slip trailing decor however, rather than the sprigging ornamentation made popular by Wedgwood. White clay slip was trailed onto the background color of the item by use of tubing to form the pattern.

Yamato — district in central Japan.

Yayoi — people of the bronze and iron culture in Japan dating back to 300-100 B.C.E. They were basically an agricultural people. They made pottery using the potter's wheel.

Yedo — or Edo, the largest city in Japan, renamed Tokyo meaning eastern capital.

Yoshihito — Emperor of Japan from 1912 to 1926. He took the name of Taisho which meant "great peace."

INDEX TO NIPPON ITEMS IN THIS BOOK

BIBLIOGRAPHY

Butler Bros. Catalogs, 1906, 1908, 1913, 1914, 1915, 1916, 1919, 1920
Ceramic Arts Co. Catalog, Trenton, N.J., circa early 1900's
Larkin Catalogs, 1916-21
Terry, Phillip, *Terry's Guide to the Japanese Empire*, Houghton Mifflin Co., Boston and New York, 1914
Thayer & Chandler Catalogs, February 15, 1918, September 1, 1918
Van Patten, Joan F., *The Nippon Primer*, 1982
Van Patten, Joan F., *The Nippon Spotter*, 1983
Van Patten, Joan F., *The Collector's Encyclopedia of Nippon Porcelain*, Collector Books, Paducah, KY., 1979
Van Patten, Joan F., *The Collector's Encyclopedia of Nippon Porcelain, Series II*, Collector Books, Paducah, KY., 1982
Van Patten, Joan F., *The Collector's Encyclopedia of Noritake*, Collector Books, Paducah, KY., 1984

Two Important Tools For The
Astute Antique Dealer, Collector and Investor

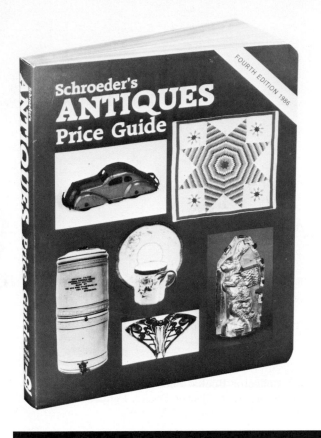

Schroeder's Antiques Price Guide

The very best low cost investment that you can make if you are really serious about antiques and collectibles is a good identification and price guide. We publish and highly recommend **Schroeder's Antiques Price Guide**. Our editors and writers are very careful to seek out and report accurate values each year. We do not simply change the values of the items each year but start anew to bring you an entirely new edition. If there are repeats, they are by chance and not by choice. Each huge edition (it weighs 3 pounds!) has over 50,000 descriptions and current values on 608 - 8½x11 pages. There are hundreds and hundreds of categories and even more illustrations. Each topic is introduced by an interesting discussion that is an education in itself. Again, no dealer, collector or investor can afford not to own this book. It is available from your favorite bookseller or antiques dealer at the low price of $9.95. If you are unable to find this price guide in your area, it's available from Collector Books, P.O. Box 3009, Paducah, KY 42001 at $9.95 plus $1.00 for postage and handling.

Flea Market Trader

Bargains are pretty hard to come by these days -- especially in the field of antiques and collectibles, and everyone knows that the most promising sources for those seldom-found under-priced treasures are flea markets. To help you recognize a bargain when you find it, you'll want a copy of the *Flea Market Trader*--the only price guide on the market that deals exclusively with all types of merchandise you'll be likely to encounter in the marketplce. It contains not only reliable pricing information, but the *Flea Market Trader* will be the first to tune you in to the market's newest collectible interests -- you will be able to buy before the market becomes established, before prices have a chance to escalate! You'll not only have the satisfaction of being first in the know, but you'll see your investments appreciate dramatically. You will love the format. Its handy 5½"x8½" size will tuck easily into pocket or purse. Its common sense organization along with detailed index makes finding your subject a breeze. There's tons of information and hundreds of photos to aid in identification. It's written with first-hand insight and an understanding of market activities. It's reliable, informative, comprehensive; it's a bargain! From Collector Books, P.O. Box 3009 Paducah, Kentucky 42001. $8.95 plus $1.00 postage and handling.

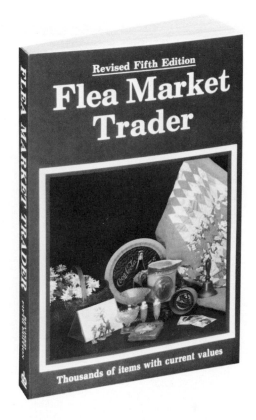